fasting
JOURNAL

fasting
JOURNAL

Jentezen Franklin

CHARISMA
HOUSE

Most CHARISMA HOUSE BOOK GROUP products are available at special quantity discounts for bulk purchase for sales promotions, premiums, fundraising, and educational needs. For details, write Charisma House Book Group, 600 Rinehart Road, Lake Mary, Florida 32746, or telephone (407) 333-0600.

FASTING JOURNAL by Jentezen Franklin
Published by Charisma House
A Charisma Media/Charisma House Book Group
600 Rinehart Road
Lake Mary, Florida 32746
www.charismahouse.com

Unless otherwise noted, all Scripture quotations are from the New King James Version of the Bible. Copyright © 1979, 1980, 1982 by Thomas Nelson, Inc., publishers. Used by permission.

Scripture quotations marked AMP are from the Amplified Bible. Old Testament copyright © 1965, 1987 by the Zondervan Corporation. The Amplified New Testament copyright © 1954, 1958, 1987 by the Lockman Foundation. Used by permission.

Scripture quotations marked KJV are from the King James Version of the Bible.

Scripture quotations marked NASU are from the New American Standard Bible—
Updated Edition, Copyright © 1960, 1962, 1963, 1968, 1971, 1972,
1973, 1975, 1977, 1995 by The Lockman Foundation. Used by permission.
(www.Lockman.org)

Scripture quotations marked NIV are from the Holy Bible, New International
Version of the Bible. Copyright © 1973, 1978, 1984, International Bible Society.
Used by permission.

Cover design by Justin Evans

Library of Congress Cataloging-in-Publication Data:
Franklin, Jentezen, 1962-
  Fasting journal / Jentezen Franklin.
      p. cm.
   ISBN 978-1-59979-386-3
  1. Fasting--Religious aspects--Christianity. I. Title.
  BV5055.F733 2008
  248.4'7--dc22

                                        2008029643

E-book ISBN: 978-1-59979-771-7

18 19 20 21 22 — 18 17 16 15 14
Printed in the United States of America

O God, You are my God;
Early will I seek You;
My soul thirsts for You;
My flesh longs for You
In a dry and thirsty land
Where there is no water.

—PSALM 63:1

As the deer pants for the water brooks,
So my soul pants for You, O God.
My soul thirsts for God, for the living God;
When shall I come and appear before God?
My tears have been my food day and night,
While they say to me all day long,
"Where is your God?"

—Psalm 42:1–3, NASU

Contents

A Personal Word From Jentezen Franklin xiii

Why Do We Fast? 1

Preparation 13

DAY

1 Getting Started 18

2 Hungering for Living Bread 22

3 Getting Past Your Quitting Point. 26

4 Target Your Prayers 30

5 Fasting and Praying 34

6 God Delights in Renewal 38

7 Feed on the Word 42

8 Walk With God 46

9 Is He Speaking to You? 50

10 Every Assignment Has a Birthplace 54

11 Fasting Truly Humbles You 58

12 The Holy Spirit Is Using Your Fast 62

13 Hold on to the Promise 66

14 Magnifying Your Worship 70

15 Renewal 74

16 Purest Worship 78

17 Nothing Is Impossible With God. 82

18 God Is Your Rock 86

19 Rewarded Openly 90

20 His Will, Not Yours 94

21 Your Final Day 98

Conclusion 103

A Personal Word From Jentezen Franklin

I AM SO GLAD YOU HAVE CHOSEN TO MAKE FASTING A PART OF your life. Fasting has been an essential part of my life and my walk with God since I was a teenager. Even in those developmental years, learning to hear His voice and see His hand move in my life, I learned that this private spiritual discipline has public rewards. To this day, when I feel myself growing spiritually dry, when I don't sense that cutting-edge anointing, when I need a fresh encounter with God, fasting is the secret key that unlocks heaven's door and slams shut the gates of hell.

The discipline of fasting releases the anointing, the favor, and the blessing of God in the life of a Christian. So if you are not content to go through this year the way you went through last year, now is the time to use the discipline of fasting to see breakthroughs. You know there's more—there's an assignment for your life, there's something God desires to release in your life, and there is a genuine desperation for those things gripping your heart. Keep these words of Jesus in mind throughout your fast:

> *Whenever* you fast, do not put on a gloomy face as the hypocrites do, for they neglect their appearance so that they will be noticed by men when they are fasting. Truly I say to you, they have their reward in full. But you, when you fast, anoint your head and wash your face so that your fasting will not be noticed by men, but by your Father who is in secret; and your Father who sees what is done in secret will reward you.
> —MATTHEW 6:16–18, NASU, EMPHASIS ADDED

There are dimensions of our glorious Lord that will never be revealed to the casual, disinterested worshiper. There are walls of intercession that will never be scaled by dispassionate religious services. But when you take steps to break out of the ordinary and worship Him as He deserves, you'll begin to see facets of His being you never knew existed. He'll begin to share secrets with you about Himself, His plans, and His desires for you. When you worship God as He deserves, He is magnified.

Your prayers take on a powerful edge when you fast. As you use this fasting and prayer devotional over the next twenty-one days, you will be amazed at the things God will show you as you press in to Him!

Why Do We Fast?

THERE ARE DIFFERENT KINDS OF FASTS. THERE ARE PRIVATE fasts that you do privately, and the Bible also describes "called fasts"—when unusual times and situations call for unusual measurements and supernatural responses from God. Here at Free Chapel we have found that the greatest time to fast is at the beginning of the year. If you give God time at the beginning of the year, He will do amazing things in your life.

There are three things you must ask yourself before you fast. Number one, what are the motives behind the fast? I appreciate the fact that you'll lose weight if you fast, but that cannot be your motive. I appreciate the fact that a fast has been proven medically to be healthy for you because it detoxifies your body, cleanses you, and causes your digestive tract to be healthier, but that is not what a fast is really all about. So, the first question you need to ask yourself is, What is my motive behind this fast? Why am I doing this? Am I doing this so I can fit back into my clothes after the Christmas holidays? That will be a side benefit, but that shouldn't be the main reason.

Second, you must ask, What are the specific needs I am fasting for? When people fasted in the Bible, they fasted for a specific need. Sometimes they were in trouble, sometimes it was for finances, and other times they were fasting for their children or for help or for direction. I want you to get in your mind the specific reasons for which you are fasting. If God came down and asked you to list the three top things you want Him to do in your life and in your family, you should know those reasons and keep them before you during the time you fast.

The third question you should ask is, Am I determined to minister unto the Lord during my fast? Acts 13:2 tells us that the prophets and teachers at the church in Antioch "ministered to the Lord and fasted." Fasting is a time we set aside for ministering to the Lord; it's not about us getting what we can get from God all the time. God will move when we fast, but it should be a time when our heart is crying out, "I want to minister to You; I want to love You; I want to know You; I want to draw closer to You; my heart cries for You."

The way you approach your fast is extremely important. If you are not serious about it, then you won't get real serious results. The more serious you are about the fast, the more serious God will respond. If you are frivolous or lighthearted about it—"Well, I'll fast, but I don't really feel like it"—that's not going to work. Your heart has to be in the fast, and when your heart is in it, there will come a fellowship with God like you have never known before!

There is an amazing Scripture verse in Zechariah 7:5: "Say to all the people of the land, and to the priests: 'When you fasted and mourned in the fifth and seventh months during those seventy years, did you really fast for Me—for Me?'" This is phenomenal. For seventy years the people had declared a certain time every year when they would fast to God. After fasting in this way for seventy years, God asked the question, "Are you fasting for Me?"

Did you know that it's possible to go on a fast and have so many personal motives and agendas that you're not even fasting unto God—you are fasting for your own wants and desires? God told the people in Zechariah's day, "You have been doing this every year at the same time for seventy years, but I want to know if anybody is hungering for Me and My kingdom, for My agenda and purpose and plan in the earth."

In the New Testament, God told the Philippian church to beware of setting their minds on "earthly things," and thus allowing their belly to become their god. (See Philippians 3:18–19.) He warned the Corinthians in this way: "And do not become idolaters as were some of them. As it is written, 'The people sat down to eat and drink, and rose up to play'" (1 Cor. 10:7). I refuse to let my belly become my god. Fasting brings the flesh off of the throne. "I discipline my body and bring it into subjection" (1 Cor. 9:27). When we fast, we submit our bodies to God and say, "Cleanse this body, and deal with the habits and other things that are earthly. Get this nicotine out of me; get this lust out of me. I'm presenting this flesh to You. I know the flesh will always be here, but I'm letting it know that Jesus is Lord in this temple."

Every time I fast, I get closer to God. Every time you fast, you will get closer to God. There is no greater reward than Him.

Biblical Fasts

There are seven types of fasts in the Bible.

1. The Esther fast—the three-day fast

In Esther 4:16 we read of the fast initiated by Queen Esther. She asked the people to "fast for me; neither eat nor drink for three days, night or day. My maids and I will fast likewise." She needed favor with the king when she stood before him. The purpose of the three-day Esther fast is to seek God's favor in the time of crisis. Are you in trouble? Is your home in trouble? Is one of your kids in trouble? Are your finances in a state of crisis? One biblical reason to fast is when there is trouble in your life.

When trouble and great crisis come, we should not fall to pieces or collapse. We don't back down when the enemy comes in. We rise up like a flood, come right back at him, and say, "You think you are bringing a crisis to me. You meant this crisis for my evil, but God is going to turn it around for my good, and this crisis is going to become a blessing." If you are in a crisis; if you are in trouble; if the crisis of depression, hopelessness, or bankruptcy is threatening you; give God a chance. Give God a chance in the time of trouble. God will turn that crisis and deliver you, just as He delivered Paul in Acts 9. When Paul was converted, the people he used to be with tried to kill him. That's what you call a *crisis*. But because he had fasted, God had a plan for his deliverance.

2. The Daniel fast—a twenty-one-day fast

The second fast is found in Daniel 10:2–3: "In those days I, Daniel, was mourning three full weeks. I ate no pleasant food, no meat or wine came into my mouth, nor did I anoint myself at all, till three whole weeks were fulfilled." This is a three-week fast, a twenty-one-day fast. This is three sevens. Seven is the number of completion.

A Daniel fast is a fast of only vegetables, fruit, and water. It includes no bread of any type, no pasta, and no meat. This will be one of the greatest, healthiest things you will ever do. Your entire system will be healthier. But why do people do the twenty-one-day fast? What result did Daniel get? After the twenty-one-day fast, Daniel said this:

> Suddenly, a hand touched me, which made me tremble on my knees and on the palms of my hands. And he said to me, "O Daniel, man greatly beloved, understand the words that I speak to you, and stand upright, for I have now been sent to you....Now I have come to make you understand what will

> happen to your people in the latter days, for the vision refers
> to many days yet to come."
>
> —DANIEL 10:10–11, 14

Just as God had a vision for Daniel, God has a vision for your life, a dream for you. He has ordered your life from beginning to end—whom you should marry, what you should do, and where you are supposed to go. He knows your every step—all of it. God has the vision. But notice that the twenty-one-day fast is what caused understanding of the vision to Daniel. Another word for understanding would be *focus* or *clarity*. It brought about the know-how to make the vision happen.

This has happened so many times in this ministry. As we've grown from one level to another, through fasting God brought us understanding of how to make the vision we had come to pass. The vision of seeing your children saved is not a lie from hell. God is not dangling the hope out there just to torment you. Habakkuk 2:3 says, "For the vision is yet for an appointed time." But you don't just wait idly for it; you do your part. And nothing positions you better for a breakthrough than a fast. God is the God of the breakthrough. Through a twenty-one-day fast, God will give you understanding of the vision He has given to you.

3. The self-examination fast—the one-day fast

In Leviticus 23:27, we read about a one-day fast: "Also the tenth day of this seventh month shall be the Day of Atonement. It shall be a holy convocation for you; you shall afflict your souls, and offer an offering made by fire to the LORD." What is this about? There is a confirming scripture in Jeremiah 36:6, which says: "Therefore go thou, and read in the roll, which thou hast written from my mouth, the words of the LORD in the ears of the people in the LORD's house upon the fasting day" (KJV). I love that: "…upon the fasting day."

In other words, God is saying, "I want you to set aside a certain time that you fast and seek Me, and here's the purpose for it—for self-examination and consecration." When you do this fast, you need to say, "God, I'm doing a checkup on me spiritually. How am I doing? Do I love You like I loved You when I first met You? Have I drawn closer to You this year, or have I lost my passion? Is my worship what You desire? Is it at the level You desire? Am I living it before my children? Is my family seeing Christ in me? What about my temper? What about my words? What about my attitude? Am I negative? Am I ugly in my actions toward people? Lord, I'm bringing myself to You because I really do want to be more like You, and I need a self-examination. I'm seeing some things in my life that are not like You, and I want You to help me deal with them on this fast." The one-day fast is a fast of self-examination.

4. The fast before a battle

There is another fast in Judges 20, which is a powerful chapter about fasting. God had told the children of Israel to fight the tribe of Benjamin, because the tribe of Benjamin had become perverted and God was ready to judge them. He said, "I want you to go fight against them."

They prayed and sought the Lord, and then asked Him, "Should we go now?"

And God said yes. He told them to send Judah up to the battle first. They sent Judah and his men to battle, and they lost the battle, losing 22,000 men. Think about what had happened; they did just what God told them to do, and it was a failure and a disaster.

They went back home and cried and sought God as earnestly as they knew how to do. Then they again asked, "Should we go out today and fight against our enemy again?"

Again, God said, "Yes, absolutely go." They went out to the battle and lost 18,000 more men. In two days, 40,000 Israeli soldiers were dead. The amazing thing is that God had told them to do it, and yet they were suffering defeat.

But then we come to verse 26, which says: "Then all the children of Israel, that is, all the people, went up and came to the house of God and wept. They sat there before the LORD and fasted that day until evening; and they offered burnt offerings and peace offerings before the LORD." The children of Israel fasted that day until evening and brought a peace offering before the Lord. If you read the rest of the story, that time they went out and completely killed off the enemy.

What is that about? You should never go into a major battle without fasting first. Don't expect to walk into expansion and do great things for God, or to start a new initiative or plan that launches you out or expands your business, without putting a day of fasting behind that effort. Something happens when we fast and pray that will not happen if you don't fast, even if God told you to do it. First, you need to attach fasting to it. It will bring the victory every time.

5. Fasting to lift God's judgment from another's life

The fifth fast is found in 1 Kings 21:27–29.

> So it was, when Ahab heard those words, that he tore his clothes and put sackcloth on his body, and fasted and lay in sackcloth, and went about mourning. And the word of the LORD came to Elijah the Tishbite, saying, "See how Ahab has

humbled himself before Me? Because he has humbled himself before Me, I will not bring the calamity in his days. In the days of his son I will bring the calamity on his house."

This is the story of Ahab, a king who was extremely wicked. A prophet prophesied over him that the dogs would lick up his blood because he had sinned against God. Do you know someone who knows right from wrong, and yet that person is living a wicked life? There is a supernatural power in fasting and prayer that is not confined just to your life.

Ahab was so wicked that the prophet told him the dogs would lick up his blood, and hearing that so moved him that he humbled himself and began to fast. God said that because that wicked man had humbled himself in fasting, God would lift the judgment. I believe that you can fast and pray and by so doing lift judgment off another's life and give them more time for God's mercy to do a work in that person's life. If you know someone for whom you desire to see God's judgment lifted, pray these words:

> Father,
> I claim this soul for You. I pray that even as I fast, You will lift judgment off _____'s life and extend mercy. Bring that person to his or her senses, I pray. Break the yoke of sin that binds. Loose the bands of wickedness. Break up and mess up ungodly associations in that person's life. Drive him or her to their knees. In Jesus's name, amen.

6. The fast for healing

Just as 1 Corinthians has become known as the "love chapter," Isaiah 58 is the "fasting chapter." In that chapter we read:

Is this not the fast that I have chosen:
To loose the bonds of wickedness,
To undo the heavy burdens,
To let the oppressed go free,
And that you break every yoke?

Is it not to share your bread with the hungry,
And that you bring to your house the poor who are cast out;
When you see the naked, that you cover him,
And not hide yourself from your own flesh?

Then your light shall break forth like the morning,
Your healing shall spring forth speedily,
And your righteousness shall go before you;
The glory of the LORD shall be your rear guard.
Then you shall call, and the LORD will answer;
You shall cry, and He will say, "Here I am."

—ISAIAH 58:6–9

This portion of Scripture says that your health will spring forth speedily. Fasting can usher in God's healing; your cholesterol levels can come down, your blood pressure can normalize, and you will feel the healing power of God come upon you. Jesus is the same yesterday, today, and forever. If we would just get out of the way and let Him be God, we will see His supernatural power at work. But we must decrease, and He must increase.

7. The dominion fast—the forty-day fast

Why did Jesus fast for forty days and forty nights? (See Matthew 4.) He did it for dominion. He did it for authority. Adam lost dominion when he ate of the fruit of the tree God told him not to eat. Esau lost his birthright by eating. In the wilderness, the children of Israel lost the Promised Land by eating quail when God had given them His supernatural provision of manna.

Is that meat you feel like eating rather than fasting worth the risk of you missing the promise of God? Fasting makes you tough in the spirit. Fasting makes the inner man rise up and say, "Devil, who do you think you are to mess with my family, or put fear in my mind, or inflict my body. Greater is He that is in me." By fasting forty days and nights, Jesus got back dominion. He returned in the power of the Spirit after He fasted.

The Effect of Godly Fasting

When you fast, you will raise up a foundation for many generations. In Ezra 8, we read these words: "Then I proclaimed a fast there at the river of Ahava, that we might humble ourselves before our God, to seek from Him the right way for us and our little ones and all our possessions" (Ezra 8:21).

I believe there are three powerful reasons indicated in this verse for fasting.

First, we fast to seek of God the right way for us. God will reveal to you the right way. He'll help you at the transitions. He'll give you the wisdom you need. He'll give you the direction that you need. You may be thinking, "Should I take that opportunity? Should I go for that job? Should I go to that college? What should I do? Should I be this or should I do that?" You should determine to fast to seek of Him the right way for yourself.

Second, you should fast for your little ones, your children. God said that you can raise up a foundation for many generations by fasting. Something begins to happen in the home of people who fast. The house of faith is built, and it extends from generation to generation to generation.

One night in Louisiana I witnessed one of the most moving things I have ever seen. I went to a church in Louisiana where there had been a perpetual prayer meeting taking place for more than thirty years. It sounds unbelievable, but there had been people praying in the church continually for more than thirty years. Not one moment had lapsed, through holidays or any other factor.

We were at that church prayer meeting at one o'clock in the morning, and six people were there in the church praying. It boggled my mind that they had been doing that not just for a year or a period of days—they had been doing this for twenty-four hours a day for more than thirty years.

The next day the pastor asked to introduce me to the person who started that prayer meeting. She was an old saint of God with gray hair pulled back into a little bun. She just looked like one of those prayer warrior grannies, if you know what I mean. After he introduced her, she laid her hands on me and prayed for me. It was a very moving experience.

Her son is now the pastor of the church. But when her son was just a young child, she made a vow to God that every year on his birthday she would shut herself in the church from sunup to sundown and call his name out in prayer. She fasted and prayed for him exclusively all day, every year, on his birthday. He was then more than fifty years old, and she had never missed his birthday.

He has become a great preacher, a great man of God. When Bill Clinton was the governor of Arkansas, he was invited to this man's church to see the Christmas play about the Messiah. He came and was so moved by it that he started flying in every year to see it. Even when he became president, he would fly down with some of his staff, and they would go to this church just to see this powerful Christmas drama. The pastor and Bill Clinton became close personal friends.

When, as the president of the United States, problems arose in the White House and he became involved in a nationally publicized moral dilemma, one of the first people Bill Clinton called was this man who had a mama who shut herself in church to fast and pray on his birthday, calling out that boy's name and asking God to use him. I believe that mother's prayer was the reason that man was able to minister to the Clintons in a powerful way.

Quit worrying about the stuff you don't like. Just know that God has somebody praying and a prayer warrior is connected to that situation. Is anybody hearing me? It just boggled my mind. Maybe that doesn't move anybody like it moves me, but to think that a mother can lock herself into a church and fast and pray and that God can take her son and call him to become the spiritual voice to the most powerful man on the planet at that time. How awesome is that!

Third, we learn in Ezra 8:21 that we should fast for substance. We fast to petition God about our substance, our resources, our finances. We affirm to God that He is our Source, and we are pleading for Him to bless us financially and materially.

Conclusion

When we fast, we are seriously seeking God's face. Fasting disrupts business as usual. Is that what you are looking for? Are you crying out for God to do something in you that He has never done before? Are you tired of business as usual?

Then, get ready to begin your fast!

A S YOU PREPARE FOR THIS INCREDIBLE TWENTY-ONE-DAY journey of fasting and prayer, there are a few things I want to impart to you.

If you do not already have one, establish a place and time where you can pray. Prayer is critical during the fast to break through and hear what the Lord is saying to you. Use this journal to keep track of your journey. You will rejoice years from now to see what amazing things have come to pass.

How do you determine what type of fast you will do for the twenty-one days? That is between you and God, and it should be a matter of prayer before you begin. You may feel led to go on a full fast in which you only drink liquids for a certain number of days—especially plenty of water. On that type of fast, you may also take in clear broth and 100 percent juices in order to maintain your strength.

Of the many different fasts mentioned in Scripture, another commonly practiced fast is the partial fast. A partial fast can be interpreted many ways. It usually involves giving up particular foods and drink for an extended period of time. The most frequently used example of a partial fast is found in the Book of Daniel, chapters 1 and 10. In the beginning of his captivity in Babylon, (Dan. 1) Daniel and three companions refused to eat the choice meats and sweets from the king's table, asking instead to have only vegetables and water. They did this for ten days to prove they would be just as healthy as the king's men.

Although you will be abstaining from food as your sacrifice, do not let the legalistic aspects of a fast crowd out the relational aspects of closeness with the Lord. He knows your heart. Closeness with the Lord is your goal, and fasting is the method to reach your goal. There are a few other things to focus on during this time that will help you maintain a "clean vessel." For example, you should refrain from critical speaking, spreading negative words about or to anyone else. Our church practices this discipline each year, and the results are amazing. Consider limiting how much you watch TV and how much time you spend on things that are distracting. Your fast will not only be a season of sacrifice, but also a season of increased warfare. You need to be at your best.

And, of course, you will enjoy many spiritual rewards of fasting, like hearing the voice of God more clearly. I love those times when it's just Jesus and me and the tears begin to flow. My favorite time is when He seems to step into the room and I am overwhelmed. I call these "sweet spots."

It is also important to have your favorite worship music available and spend time worshiping often. And if possible, I highly recommend establishing some form of accountability during the fast, either with someone who is fasting with you, or a prayer partner.

In Daniel chapter 10, Daniel was grieved and burdened with the revelation he'd received for Israel. He ate no choice breads or meats and drank no wine for three weeks. Then he described the angel that was sent to him—but had been delayed by the prince of Persia for twenty-one days—with the answers Daniel sought. His fast broke the power of the delayer and released the angels of God so that God's purposes could be revealed and served.

Whenever you begin a fast, remember, if it doesn't mean anything to you, it won't mean anything to God. Without being combined with prayer and the Word, fasting is little more than dieting. But I want you to realize something very important: Fasting itself is a continual prayer before God.

There may be days when heaven opens and your heart is prompted to deep times of prayer. But there may be other days when your energy is sapped and you just cannot seem to focus in prayer at all. Don't condemn yourself. God sees your sacrifice.

My Twenty-One-Day Fast Begins Today!

I commit to fast from (date) _____ to (date) _____

The reason I am fasting:

_____

_____

_____

_____

What am I fasting from?

_____

_____

_____

_____

The results of my fast:

_____

_____

_____

_____

WHAT IS FASTING? Since there are so many misconceptions about it, I first want to clarify what fasting—biblical fasting—is not. Fasting is not merely going without food for a period of time. That is starving—maybe even dieting—but fasting it is not. Nor is fasting something done only by a bunch of fanatics. I really want to drive that point home. Fasting is not to be done only by religious monks alone in a cave somewhere. The practice of fasting is not limited to ministers or to special occasions.

Stated simply, biblical fasting is refraining from food for a spiritual purpose. Fasting has always been a normal part of a relationship with God. As expressed by the impassioned plea of David in Psalm 42, fasting brings one into a deeper, more intimate, and more powerful relationship with the Lord.

When you eliminate food from your diet for a number of days, your spirit becomes uncluttered by the things of this world and amazingly sensitive to the things of God. As David stated, "Deep calls unto deep" (Ps. 42:7). David was fasting. His hunger and thirst for God were greater than his natural desire for food. As a result, he reached a place where he could cry out from the depths of his spirit to the depths of God, even in the midst of his trial. Once you've experienced even a glimpse of that kind of intimacy with our God—our Father, the holy Creator of the universe—and the countless rewards and blessings that follow, your whole perspective will change. You will soon realize that fasting is a secret source of power that is overlooked by many.

> A threefold cord is not quickly broken.
> —ECCLESIASTES 4:12

During the years that Jesus walked this earth, He devoted time to teaching His disciples the principles of the kingdom of God, principles that conflict with those of this world. In the Beatitudes, specifically in Matthew 6,

Jesus provided the pattern by which each of us is to live as a child of God. That pattern addressed three specific duties of a Christian: giving, praying, and fasting. Jesus said, *"When you give..."* and *"When you pray..."* and *"When you fast."* He made it clear that fasting, like giving and praying, was a normal part of Christian life. As much attention should be given to fasting as is given to giving and to praying.

Fasting brings you into a deeper, more intimate, and more powerful relationship with the Lord. You are on your way!

> When God has placed a dream inside you
>
> that only He can make possible, you need
>
> to fast and pray. Good or bad, what's in you
>
> will come out only when you fast and pray.

On your first day of fasting, remember:

- Pray and stay in God's Word.
- Drink lots of water.
- Expect headaches; hunger pangs; and cravings for food, sugar, and caffeine.
- Play praise and worship music as much as possible.

Thoughts for your journal:

- ◇ What are your own personal reasons for fasting?
- ◇ Do you desire sensitivity to the things of God?

_____

_____

_____

_____

_____

_____

PRAYER FOCUS DAY 1: Salvation of Souls

THERE IS NO greater burden for which to seek the Lord than the salvation of souls. If you have unsaved friends and family—and we all do—they need to hear of God's love for them, but they also need to understand that there is a very real, very dark, very horrific place for those who do not accept Jesus. The Lord spoke more of *hell* than He did of *heaven*. So, as you begin this fast, let your focus be the souls of those close to you who need salvation. Do not be discouraged but persistent. Keep praying! "Consider him who endured such opposition from sinful men, so that you will not grow weary and lose heart" (Heb. 12:3, NIV).

My spiritual "hit list"

Unsaved family members and friends to target in prayer during this fast. Write their names in the spaces below:

_____	_____	_____
_____	_____	_____
_____	_____	_____
_____	_____	_____
_____	_____	_____
_____	_____	_____
_____	_____	_____

> I tell you, now is the time of God's favor, now is the day of salvation.
> —2 Corinthians 6:2, NIV

TOO MANY CHRISTIANS find that they are malnourished in the Word of God but well fed on the world, and they live defeated lives as a result.

Where does the kind of faith come from that enables you to look to God and believe His Word no matter how grave your circumstances may *appear*? Your daughter is unsaved and on drugs. Your father lies dying in a hospital bed. You are about to be evicted from the house you rent because it's been sold out from under you. Your marriage of twenty years has come to an end, and the divorce papers have been signed. I could go on and on. These are very real circumstances that have no solution in the natural. Where does such faith come from?

"Faith comes by hearing, and hearing by the word of God" (Rom. 10:17). The Amplified version of this Scripture verse states, "Faith comes by hearing [what is told], and what is heard comes by the preaching [of the message that came from the lips] of Christ (the Messiah Himself)." It is by hearing God's Word, by hearing the preaching of the gospel, that faith increases. There is something about getting in a church where the anointing flows and you hear the Word of God preached. Faith does not come from programs, dynamite worship teams, or being with a group of people who are like you. Faith comes when you hear a man or woman of God preach the Word without compromise to all who will listen. That is the birthplace of faith. If this revelation truly takes hold of your spirit, you will never allow the devil to talk you out of being faithful to God's house.

In the introduction of *Fasting*, I mentioned how Eve saw that the fruit was good for food. God's Word to Adam and Eve was, "In the day that you eat of it you will surely die" (Gen. 2:17). Yet Eve acted on the wisdom of the world that was spoken by the serpent instead of walking away in faith that God's Word was true.

In contrast, as Jesus fasted in the desert, He was tempted by the same voice that had so cunningly whispered to Eve. Yet Jesus responded, "Man shall not live by bread alone, but by every word that proceeds from the mouth of God" (Matt. 4:4). What had Jesus heard just before beginning that time of fasting? "And lo a voice from heaven, saying, This is my beloved Son, in whom I am well pleased" (Matt. 3:17, KJV). The Word of God sustained Him through forty days and nights without food.

How I wish the body of Christ today had that same kind of hunger for God's Word. I would love to see the day when, if a Christian had to, he or she would go to church in pajamas rather than miss *hearing* God's Word! I know that sounds extreme, but we live in extreme times. We need to understand Jesus's words when He said, "Heaven and earth will pass away, but My words will by no means pass away" (Mark 13:31).

In anything you do, the first step is the most difficult, but as you walk through this twenty-one-day journey, you will find that God is there to meet you at every critical point along the way.

> The Son of God fasted because He knew
> there were supernatural things that could be
> released only that way. How much more should
> fasting be a common practice in our lives?

On your second day of fasting, remember:

◊ Pray and stay in God's Word.

- ◇ Rest to conserve your energy.
- ◇ The second and third days are the most challenging.
- ◇ Your body starts burning fat for energy, a process called "ketosis."

Thoughts for your journal:

- ◇ Do you need a deeper, more intimate, and more powerful relationship with the Lord?
- ◇ Do you need a fresh encounter with God?

PRAYER FOCUS DAY 2: Pastors

YOUR PASTOR —ALL pastors — need prayer. Sometimes the weight of ministry can get so overwhelming that the joy, freshness, and power of the calling can be forgotten. As with Elijah, the spirit of Jezebel attempts to ensnare through lust and pride, and if that doesn't work, it brings discouragement and defeat. (See 1 Kings 18–19.) The attacks affect not only pastors, but often their families as well.

Fasting and praying for protection, restored joy, and increased anointing in your pastor's life will release untold blessings on him, your church, and even your own life. If you know of specific areas you could target in prayer, list them below.

Specific prayer points for my pastor and his family:

_____

_____

_____

_____

_____

> Now may the God of peace who
> brought up our Lord Jesus from the
> dead, that great Shepherd of the sheep,
> through the blood of the everlasting
> covenant, make you complete in every
> good work to do His will, working
> in you what is well pleasing in His
> sight, through Jesus Christ, to whom
> be glory forever and ever. Amen.
> —Hebrews 13:20–21

FASTING STIRS A hunger in your spirit that goes deeper than any temporary hunger you experience in your flesh. When you *hunger* for God, He will fill you! Jesus went through cities where He could do no miracles—because there was no hunger. In this day, God is saying, "I'm looking for somebody who wants something. I'm looking for somebody who will do more than show up for another church service, but they will hunger for that which I want to place in them!"

Why is fasting so often overlooked? I believe the primary reason is one that has plagued mankind since the dawn of creation.

You see, fasting means crucifying what I refer to as "King Stomach." And in case you don't know who King Stomach is, just move this book out of the way, look down, and introduce yourself. You've probably already heard him rumble in disagreement a time or two since you began reading this book!

It has been said that the way to a man's heart is through his stomach. Most women have come to know it, but we need to realize that the devil knows it too! Some people—specifically Christians—could be the geographical location of the "bottomless pit"! Consider for just a moment what has happened to the human race while under the rule of King Stomach.

We can start at the beginning, all the way back in the Garden of Eden to the time when the serpent was cunning and convinced Eve that she should eat from the forbidden tree, assuring her that she would not die. "So when the woman saw that the tree was good for food…she took of its fruit and ate. She also gave to her husband with her, and he ate" (Gen. 3:6).

And with that one meal, Adam and Eve immediately went from peacefully enjoying God's presence in the cool of the garden to fearfully hiding from His presence among the trees of the garden.

They literally ate themselves out of house and home. They ate themselves out of the will of God for their lives. They ate themselves out of God's provision and plan for their lives and out of His magnificent presence. But their stomachs were temporarily satisfied, and we still suffer the consequences of their appetites today.

When speaking of the sins of Sodom and Gomorrah, people usually focus on the rampant homosexuality in those cities. But that is not all the Bible teaches. The Lord said to Israel through the prophet Ezekiel: "Look, this was the iniquity of your sister Sodom: She and her daughter had pride, fullness of food, and abundance of idleness; neither did she strengthen the hand of the poor and needy. And they were haughty and committed abomination before Me; therefore I took them away as I saw fit" (Ezek. 16:49–50).

The first thing you may notice is that there was no giving (to the poor and needy) and no praying, which indicates pride and idleness. But it is interesting to note that the inhabitants of those cities were not only guilty of homosexuality according to the account in Genesis, but as we see here, they were guilty of gluttony (fullness of food). Along with their other sins, their excessive loyalty to King Stomach carried them right into damnation!

On this the third day, you are passing a crucial hurdle on your way to your twenty-one-day goal. So don't give up—stay hungry!

> Like Jesus told the disciples at the well in Samaria, when
> you open yourself to know the will of the Father and
> do the will of the Father, no steak or cake compares.
> Nothing can fill you and satisfy you like that.

On your third day of fasting, remember:

- ◇ Pray for encouragement.
- ◇ This is usually the toughest day of the fast.
- ◇ Noticeable weight loss begins.

Thoughts for your journal:

- ◇ What is the Holy Spirit showing you about endurance?
- ◇ What dreams are in your heart that only God can make possible?

PRAYER FOCUS DAY 3: Direction, Guidance, Dreams, and Visions

DURING THIS FAST, seek God for direction and guidance in your life. Paul said, "I was not disobedient to the heavenly vision" (Acts 26:19). Vision comes from God to help you and other people and to establish His kingdom in the earth (not to be confused with ambition, which comes from the flesh and is self seeking). Remember the six stages of a vision:

- ◇ *I thought it*—God gives you the vision.
- ◇ *I caught it*—you start to get excited about the vision.

- ◊ *I bought it*—you consider the cost of the vision and pay the price.

- ◊ *I sought it*—nobody can talk you out of it.

- ◊ *I got it*—you actually possess the dream and are glad you paid the price to get it.

- ◊ *I taught it*—you pass it on to the next generation.

Never settle for less than God's best for your life! As God instructed Habakkuk: "Write the vision and make it plain on tablets…though it tarries, wait for it" (Hab. 2:2–3). What vision has God given you? Write it down and focus on it during the fast.

> The steps of a good man are ordered by
> the LORD, and He delights in his way.
> —Psalm 37:23

P AUL SAID THE weapons of our warfare are "mighty through God to the pulling down of strong holds" (2 Cor. 10:4, KJV). And such weapons need to be honed to properly hit the target. In Matthew 17, the disciples were frustrated because they could not cast the demon out of the boy. Jesus explained, "This kind does not go out except by prayer and fasting" (v. 21). Among other things, fasting helps you to focus and target your prayers more effectively.

I love the statement Jesus made in John 10:27: "My sheep *hear* My voice" (emphasis added). That is how He created us. He speaks to us, and we are able to hear Him speaking. Do you want to hear the voice of the Creator? Do you want to know Jesus more deeply? Do you want to know the direction He desires you to take in life? I do.

As I was completing my book *Fasting*, I was beginning my fifth twenty-one-day fast since entering the ministry. I began my first one when I was just seventeen years old. My parents were always godly examples when I was growing up, so even at that young age I was becoming aware that fasting was a part of being a true follower of Christ. If you are a parent reading this book, I want you to know that even children can begin to understand these concepts, and it is important that they learn them at a young age.

Prior to that first twenty-one-day fast at the age of seventeen, I had completed shorter ones. In fact, it was during a three-day fast that God revealed His assignment for my life. I was praying and seeking His will. That is when He called me to preach.

Recently, the Lord shared something with me that I believe will help you as you desire to hear His voice and know His will. He said simply, "Every assignment has a birthplace." Every assignment, every call of God, every direction from Him starts somewhere. God has specific assignments for your life. But how do you discover them? How will you hear His voice? How will you know His will for your life, His plans for you? Whom should you marry? Where should you live? What job should you take? What mission field is calling your name?

The answer can be found in the appeal Paul made to the Romans: "Present your bodies a living sacrifice, holy, acceptable to God, which is your reasonable service" (Rom. 12:1). Remember the three Christian duties I covered in day 1? Giving, praying, and *fasting*. That is how you "present" your body to God as a "living" sacrifice. Fasting keeps you sensitive to His Spirit, enabling you to live holy. Paul went on to say, "And do not be conformed to this world, but be transformed by the renewing of your mind, *that you may prove what is that good and acceptable and perfect will of God*" (Rom. 12:2, emphasis added).

I am convinced that we will never walk in the perfect will of God until we seek Him through fasting. When you present your body in this manner, you open yourself up to hear from God. You will prove or discover His good and perfect will for your life. Paul was fasting when God called him and shared the assignment for his life (Acts 9:7–9). Peter was fasting on the rooftop when God gave him a new revelation and called him to take the gospel to the Gentiles (Acts 10). Fasting prepares the way for God to give you fresh revelation, fresh vision, and clear purpose.

In the Book of Joel, the Lord said, "And it shall come to pass afterward that I will pour out My Spirit on all flesh; your sons and your daughters shall prophesy, your old men shall dream dreams, your young men shall see visions" (Joel 2:28). God was going to pour out revival—*afterward*. He was revealing His will for His people—afterward. After what? After a fast. Israel was in sin, and God was calling His people to fast in repentance as a people: "Blow the trumpet in Zion, consecrate a *fast*, call a sacred assembly" (Joel 2:15, emphasis added). His promise to them was to pour out revival and blessings on the land. I don't know about you, but I'm ready for those "afterward" seasons when God pours out revival, when our sons and daughters prophesy!

What are we waiting for when we read scriptures like 2 Chronicles 7:14? Can you imagine if believers in America really took hold of this, if they humbled themselves (fasted) and prayed? God would heal our nation and send revival!

But if He is going to pour out new wine, our wineskins will have to change. Jesus said, "No one puts new wine into old wineskins; or else the new wine bursts the wineskins, the wine is spilled, and the wineskins are ruined. But new wine must be put into new wineskins" (Mark 2:22). I had never seen the connection between fasting and the new wine before. But if you look at this passage, Jesus had just finished telling the Pharisees that His disciples would fast once He was gone. Fasting is what prepares you for a new anointing (Mark 2:20). God can't put that kind of wine in old skins. If you want new wine, new miracles, new closeness, new intimacy with Him, then it's time to call a fast and shed that old skin for the new.

> Fasting prepares the way for God to give you
> fresh revelation, fresh vision, and clear purpose.

On your fourth day of fasting, remember:

◊ Listen as you pray.

◊ Record His response to your prayers.

◊ You begin to settle into the fast.

Thoughts for your journal:

◊ Is there any healing that you need physically?

◊ What are the needs in your family right now?

PRAYER FOCUS DAY 4: Intercessors

YOU ARE A spiritual "gatekeeper" in your home, your family, and your city. Your intercessory prayers for these areas help maintain a wall of protection against demonic attack. Interceding is intervening, or stepping in on behalf of another. Even people who would never speak to you in person have no defense against your prayers. Your prayers can go into bars. Your prayers can go into crack houses. Your prayers can go anywhere. E. M. Bounds said, "Prayers outlive the lives of those who uttered them." Spend today focusing on your own intercessory prayer life, praying for other intercessors, and praying that God would raise up more intercessors. We need prayers that will outlive our generation!

Intercessory targets for my family, my city, and my country:

And pray in the Spirit on all occasions
with all kinds of prayers and requests.
With this in mind, be alert and always
keep on praying for all the saints.
—Ephesians 6:18, NIV

JESUS, WHILE BEING a very public figure, was actually a very private person. You do not see Him praying in public nearly as much as you see Him praying in private. In fact, our Savior was so committed to private prayer that He would often pray for hours on end, even all through the night. He seemed to crave intimate moments alone with His Father in heaven. But if Jesus could have accomplished all He came to do by praying alone, why would He fast?

Could we be missing our greatest breakthroughs because we fail to fast? Remember the thirtyfold, sixtyfold, and hundredfold return Jesus spoke of (Mark 4:8, 20)? Look at it this way: when you pray, you can release that thirtyfold return, but when both prayer and giving are part of your life, I believe that releases the sixtyfold blessing. But when all three—giving, praying, and fasting—are part of your life, that hundredfold return can be released!

If that's the case, you have to wonder what blessings are not being released. What answers to prayer are not getting through? What bondages are not being broken because we fail to fast?

Matthew tells the story of a father who had a demon-possessed son. For years he watched helplessly as his son suffered with severe convulsions. As he grew older, the attacks became so severe that the boy would often throw himself into an open fire or a trench of water. A suicidal spirit tormented him constantly; the situation became life-threatening.

Having exhausted every attempt to cure the boy—even taking him to the disciples—with no avail, the father's plight seemed impossible. Then he heard that Jesus was near. Going to the Master, he cried, "Lord, have mercy on my son: for he is lunatick, and sore vexed: for ofttimes he falleth into the fire, and oft into the water. And I brought him to thy disciples, and they could not cure him" (Matt. 17:15, KJV).

When the boy was brought to Jesus, the Bible says He "rebuked the devil;

and he departed out of him: and the child was cured from that very hour" (v. 18, KJV). But what made the difference? After all, Matthew 10:1 records that Jesus had already given the disciples power to cast out evil spirits and to heal every disease. So why couldn't the disciples cast out the demon and cure the boy?

That's what they wanted to know too, so later that night, when they were alone with Jesus, they asked Him. Jesus replied, "Because of your unbelief: for verily I say unto you, If ye have faith as a grain of mustard seed, ye shall say unto this mountain, Remove hence to yonder place; and it shall remove; and nothing shall be impossible unto you. Howbeit this kind goeth not out but by prayer and fasting" (Matt. 17:20–21).

Now, I've read that passage many times, and I've even taught from it on occasion. But each time, I've focused on the statement "nothing shall be impossible unto you." I think a lot of people stop right there, but Jesus didn't because He knew there was more—much more.

See, that funny little word *howbeit* is the connection—it's the key that unlocks the power in the statement "nothing shall be impossible unto you." Jesus told the disciples they needed faith, even faith as small as a tiny seed. But that wasn't all. Long before this incident, the Holy Spirit led Jesus into the wilderness, where He spent forty days and forty nights, taking no food. "Howbeit this kind goeth not out but by prayer and fasting." For Jesus, casting out that stubborn demon wasn't impossible.

If Jesus could have accomplished all He came to do without fasting, why would He fast? The Son of God fasted because He knew there were supernatural things that could be released only that way. How much more should fasting be a common practice in our lives?

If you are ready to bring supernatural blessings into your life and release the power of God to overcome any situation, begin today making the discipline of fasting a part of your life. You will be greatly rewarded!

On your fifth day of fasting, remember:

- ◊ Journal your journey.
- ◊ Concentrate on your own personal prayer time and prayer place.
- ◊ Headaches and cravings begin to subside.
- ◊ Bad breath becomes apparent as your body detoxifies.

Thoughts for your journal:

- ◊ Why do you think fasting is important in order to achieve your greatest breakthroughs?
- ◊ Jesus fasted, and He intimately related to His Father in heaven. How has this fast, so far, helped you to relate to your heavenly Father?

AKE TIME TODAY to thank God that Jesus is your healer. If there is sickness in your body or mind, or in the body or mind of a loved one, begin to speak forth health and healing in Jesus's name. Begin to declare: "By His stripes I *am* healed....With long life You will satisfy me and my family, and show me Your salvation." (See Isaiah 53:5; Psalm 91:16.) Just begin to speak it out loud because you reap what you speak. By your words and prayers, release health and healing over your body, your family, your church, and your city. May the name of Jehovah-Rapha, the healing One, be proclaimed in this generation!

Specific healing targets:

_____

_____

_____

_____

_____

> But to you who fear My name
> the Sun of Righteousness shall
> arise with healing in His wings.
> —Malachi 4:2

DAY 6: God Delights in Renewal

SOMETIMES WE NEED renewal in our spiritual lives. Fasting is one of the ways you can cleanse your body and aid the process of communicating with the Father. God is already raising up people in this hour who do not want a diet of just "church as normal" any longer. Hungry people are desperate people.

If we are not careful, we can allow life to get us into the same old ruts and routines without even realizing it. Our relationships with the Lord can suffer the same fate. When we don't do what it takes to stay sharp and sensitive to the Holy Spirit, our praise, worship, offerings, and even preaching can become heartless routines to God. As a believer, you can pray, read your Bible, and go to church week after week and still be losing sight of your first love. It is not that you don't love the Lord, but the business of life can bring you to the point of losing your freshness, your enthusiasm, and your sensitivity to His Spirit and what pleases Him.

My mother was an excellent cook. But if she had gotten so caught up in other things that all she ever put on the table for us was meatloaf every night of the week, I don't think it would have taken long for me to find somewhere else to eat. The disappointing sound of comments like, "Aw, Mom, meatloaf again?" would have been common at my house. What if God were hungry and all we have to feed Him is our same dull religious routines day after day? Just like ending up with meatloaf on the table every night, I can just hear our heavenly Father sighing, "Religion again?"

That's why God said to Israel, "If I were hungry, I would not tell you; for the world is Mine, and all its fullness" (Ps. 50:12). God owns the cattle on a thousand hills. He does not need our routines. He does not savor heartless activity. He does not want our "leftovers" when He can get "fed" elsewhere. True worship that comes from our hearts feeds Him and satisfies Him; it is something He desires—and deserves. Our religiosity of going through the motions once a week does not please Him as much as our obedience to His Word.

The reason this subject fits in a book about fasting is simple: fasting is a constant means of renewing yourself spiritually. The discipline of fasting breaks you out of the world's routine. It is a form of worship—offering your body to God as a living sacrifice is holy and pleasing to God (Rom. 12:1). The discipline of fasting will humble you, remind you of your dependency on God, and bring you back to your first love. It causes the roots of your relationship with Jesus to go deeper.

There are dimensions of our glorious King that will never be revealed to the casual, disinterested worshiper. There are walls of intercession that will never be scaled by dispassionate religious service. But when you take steps to break out of the ordinary and worship Him as He deserves, you will begin to see facets of His being you never knew existed. He will begin to share secrets with you about Himself, His plans, His desires for you. When you worship God as He deserves, He is magnified.

When you are truly hungry for God, you will push past the customs, you will push over the rituals—you don't want to leave hungry!

> Don't allow the enemies in your life to cause you to focus more on your appetite or circumstances than on the promises of God that are released when you employ the powerful weapon of fasting.

On your sixth day of fasting, remember:

⬦ Concentrate on prolonged times of meditation and listening.

⬦ Your senses (smell, touch, hearing) will begin to heighten.

⬦ Weight loss and detoxification continue.

Thoughts for your journal:

⬦ How is experiencing fasting as a private discipline bringing you closer to God?

⬦ Has God revealed anything to you since your fast began?

_____

_____

_____

_____

_____

_____

_____

_____

_____

_____

YOU CANNOT ENJOY the fullness of life in Christ when you are still a slave, bound by addictions. Sexual and chemical addictions like alcohol and drugs, nicotine, overeating, antidepressants, insomnia, and so on can be broken through the discipline of fasting. If there are addictions in your life, list them below and ask God to give you grace during this fast to walk away free of those chains! Perhaps there is a family member or loved one suffering with addiction. Write down his or her name to target for prayer during this time.

_____

_____

_____

_____

_____

_____

_____

So if the Son sets you free,
you will be free indeed.
—John 8:36, NIV

DAY 7: Feed on the Word

J ESUS SAID, "BLESSED are those who hunger and thirst for righteousness, for they shall be filled" (Matt. 5:6). When you begin to develop a hunger for the deeper things of God, He will fill you. As Job proclaimed, "I have not departed from the commandment of His lips; I have treasured the words of His mouth more than my necessary food" (Job 23:12).

We must diligently feed on God's Word. Sometimes the best thing we can possibly do is starve our flesh and feed our spirit through a fast. Fasting helps you separate what you *want* from what you *need*. It causes you to focus on those things that really matter.

Believe me, fasting allows you many opportunities to diligently seek the Lord! You diligently seek Him when everyone else is going out to the movies, drinking sodas, and eating popcorn and you choose to stay home to be with the Lord because you just *have* to hear from Him. Diligently seeking Him through fasting happens in the morning when everyone else gets up and eats bacon, eggs, pancakes, real maple syrup, grits, hash browns, and fried sausage and you choose to spend time with God. It comes when you're at work and everyone else is having burgers, fries, and shakes for lunch, but you are having bottled water! Diligence is when you come home from a long, hard day at work, and all you have had all day is water, yet you separate yourself from the dinner table to feed on the Word.

To be diligent is to be persistent. It means to work hard in doing something and refusing to stop. God delivered the Israelites from Pharaoh's slavery. He parted the Red Sea so they could cross on dry ground, but He allowed Pharaoh's army to drown. Yet, the children of Israel got out into the wilderness and started complaining. After all He had done for them, they were still not diligent about seeking the Lord, and that older generation never entered into His rest, His reward.

Faith is progressive. Faith never gets into a bad situation and says, "I'm just going to sit here and die. It's over." Faith never stands in the desert, having a pity party with everything drying up around it. You walk by faith. You don't stand still, drowning in your misery. When you get in a wilderness, you keep walking; you keep going forward even if you are only making an inch of progress with each step. When you get into battles, you have to keep saying, "I will move forward."

When a reward is offered for someone's capture, the reward is provided before it is claimed. The money is placed into an account to be held until the offender is captured. God is a rewarder of those who diligently seek Him (Heb. 11:6), which means He has already laid up rewards for you in heaven. In my mind, when reading this scripture, I've always added, "seek Him…and find Him." That is not what it says. The Bible tells us that if we *seek*, we will *find*.

> Too many Christians find that they are malnourished in the Word but well fed on the world, and they live defeated lives as a result.

On your seventh day of fasting, remember:

- ◊ Water needs to be with you at all times.
- ◊ Rest and relax as much as possible.
- ◊ Continue to meditate and listen.

Thoughts for your journal:

- ◇ How are you resisting the temptation of hunger?
- ◇ How can resisting hunger by focusing on the Lord relate to avoiding other temptations in your life?

PRAYER FOCUS DAY 7: Finances and Prosperity

G OD HAS TOLD us through His Word that when we acknowledge Him in all of our ways and lean not on our own understanding, He will direct our paths (Prov. 3:6). That includes finances. On this seventh day of your fast, ask God to set things aright in your finances. Sow a "firstfruits offering." If you sow the unusual, you will release an unusual harvest back into your life. Expect financial miracles this year! Seek Him for blessings and prosperity that can be used to advance and expand His kingdom and bless others. You take care of the little things, and God will handle the big things. Don't worry about the money; just do what God tells you to do. He's the God of provision; He will see to it; He will provide; He will make a way. Even if you're looking at something that seems bigger than you, boldly declare it right now: "Thank You, Lord, for being my Provider in all things. I give You praise for provision! Thank You, Father."

Specific financial needs to hold up in prayer today:

_____

_____

_____

_____

_____

_____

_____

_____

> But remember the LORD your God,
> for it is he who gives you the ability
> to produce wealth, and so confirms
> his covenant, which he swore to
> your forefathers, as it is today.
> —Deuteronomy 8:18, NIV

CAN YOU IMAGINE what it must have been like to be Adam or Eve, walking with our glorious God in the peace of the garden? Tragedy of tragedies—they chose to give up that glorious place for something to eat! Fasting prepares the way for God to communicate clearly with you, to give you fresh revelations, fresh visions, and clear purpose. You are already past the seventh day. Do not grow weary. Stay the course; finish the race. An incredible reward awaits you on the other side.

Jesus said, "Blessed are those who hunger and thirst for righteousness, for they shall be filled" (Matt. 5:6). When you begin to develop a hunger for the deeper things of God, He will fill you. However, sometimes just being in a good service is not enough. I believe God is already raising up people in this hour who do not want a diet of just "church as normal" any longer. I see it at Free Chapel; people are fasting and developing a hunger for more of God, and religious traditions are having to just get out of the way. Hungry people are desperate people. They will push over the custom; they will push over the ritual—they don't want to leave hungry.

Jesus found such hunger while visiting Tyre and Sidon. A woman whose daughter was possessed and tormented by a devil heard that He was there. But the woman was Greek, "a Syro-Phoenician by birth" (Mark 7:26), and, therefore, outside of the covenant God had made with Israel. But that didn't matter to her. She was hungry, and her faith was persistent. Even when Jesus discouraged her, saying that the "bread" was first for the children of Israel, she was hungry enough to ask for even a crumb that would fall to the floor. Many of the children who sat at the table had not shown such great hunger. Jesus honored her request, and her daughter was healed because of her persistence (vv. 29–30).

Hungry people are desperate people, and they are hungry for more of God than they have ever had. They are breaking out of religious rules, regulations, and traditional thinking and breaking through to more of His presence, more of His power to turn situations around, more of His healing power, and more of His miracle-working power! Only Jesus satisfies that hunger!

It was such hunger that was stirred in the heart of a Gentile centurion in Caesarea who fasted, prayed to God always, and gave generously to the poor. Though they were Gentiles, Cornelius and his household devoutly feared and served God. As Cornelius was fasting and praying one day like Daniel, an angel appeared to him with a message. The angel said, "Your prayers and your alms have come up for a memorial before God" (Acts 10:4). And then the angel instructed him to send for Peter, who was nearby in Joppa. Peter, who was fasting at the time as well, saw a vision from God in which many foods that were unlawful for Jews to eat were presented to him. He was still puzzled by the vision when Cornelius's messengers arrived. Going with them to his house the next day and hearing of the hunger in this man's heart, Peter understood that the vision meant that the gospel was not to be withheld from the Gentiles. As he shared the gospel with those of Cornelius's house-hold, the Holy Spirit fell and baptized them all, and later they were baptized in water. (See Acts 10.)

When you hunger for God, He will fill you. As Jesus entered Capernaum, He was confronted by a Roman centurion whose servant was paralyzed and tormented (Matt. 8:5–13). But the centurion knew it would take only a word from Jesus for the servant to be healed. When he said those words to Jesus, the Bible says Jesus was amazed at his faith and told those around him, "I have not found such great faith, not even in Israel!" (v. 10). He was saying, "So many in Abraham's lineage don't have the hunger this man has shown. They come to see Me, but they don't hunger." In this day, God is saying, "I'm looking for somebody who wants something. I'm looking for somebody who will do more than show up, but who will hunger for that which I want to place in him!"

> In this day, God is saying, "I'm looking for somebody who wants something. I'm looking for somebody who will do more than show up, but who will hunger for that which I want to place in him!"

On your eighth day of fasting, remember:

- ◊ Pray and stay in God's Word.
- ◊ You begin to discover what is known as the "sweet spot"—a place you hit that will be as though you slipped through the veil and walked right into the holy of holies.

Thoughts for your journal:

- ◊ Reflect on how there is great power and supernatural blessing that await you as you forsake all flesh for the chance to know the Savior and to hear His voice.

MARRIAGE DOESN'T TAKE two people; it takes three. You cannot have a good marriage if God is not in the center of it. And that applies to those who are single as well. Your courting days should be centered on Christ and purity, establishing a firm foundation for the future. Today, if you are married, cover your spouse and your marriage with prayer. Pray for others in your family and circle of friends who are married. Marriage is under attack by the enemy in this country! If you are single, pray that God will bring you His utmost choice for your life, and commit to settle for nothing less.

Praying for marriage:

_____

_____

_____

_____

_____

> Nevertheless let each one of you
> in particular so love his own wife
> as himself, and let the wife see
> that she respects her husband.
> —Ephesians 5:33

A T THIS POINT you should become more aware of the Lord's presence all around you. Your hunger for His provision and His attention has intensified.

When we fast according to His plan, God says, "Then you shall call, and the LORD will answer; you shall cry, and He will say, 'Here I am'" (Isa. 58:9). Remember what the angel told Daniel in Daniel 10? From the first day that Daniel began to fast, God heard. The only thing that held up his answer was battle in the heavens!

A woman who volunteers for Free Chapel gave the most amazing testimony to this fact. Her parents had been in severe financial trouble for over a year. They had been given notice of foreclosure proceedings if they did not pay $5,500. She called her unsaved brothers and asked them if they wanted to join her in doing something that would help her parents in this desperate situation. God backed her up! Her brothers agreed, and they began to fast. Within fifteen days of the house being foreclosed, her parents received a phone call. Her father had applied for disability in 2000, but it took six years for them to get around to having the hearing on his case. They called to inform the family that his disability application had been approved, and a check was in the mail that very day in the amount of—are you ready for this?—$86,000, which included the amount from 2000. In addition, he would be getting disability payments monthly. There is no way her brothers can deny that God is the One who brought about this miracle.

God's promises don't stop there. He also says:

> Then shall thy light rise in obscurity, and thy darkness be as the noonday: and the LORD shall guide thee continually, and satisfy thy soul in drought, and make fat thy bones: and thou shalt be like a watered garden, and like a spring of water,

whose waters fail not. And they that shall be of thee shall build the old waste places: thou shalt raise up the foundations of many generations.

—ISAIAH 58:10–12, KJV

Your light will rise out of obscurity. In other words, in situations you face that are just overwhelming and you don't know how to find your way through the darkness of obscurity and confusion, God will cause your light to shine on the path you are to take.

Though the path before you may be obscure, when you fast and pray in faith, God will reward you and guide you. "Your ears shall hear a word behind you, saying, 'This is the way, walk in it'" (Isa. 30:21).

Remember, it was during a fast that Paul received the call of God and the assignment for his life. Peter was fasting when he received his "rooftop revelation" from the Lord, who called Peter to take the gospel to the Gentiles. What will God reveal to you during your fast?

> Maybe you have rebellious children or sons
> and daughters who are committing fornication,
> but I'm telling you, fasting and praying will
> absolutely break those spirits off their lives.

On your ninth day of fasting, remember:

◊ Maintain your journal.

- ◇ Continue to meditate and listen.
- ◇ Mints will keep your breath fresh.

Thoughts for your journal:

- ◇ Reflect on the battle that ensues between the carnal man and the spirit.
- ◇ How has God's presence become more clear through this experience?

_____

_____

_____

_____

_____

PRAYER FOCUS DAY 9: Family

NO MATTER WHERE I go, I never go by myself. What I mean is, I carry with me part of the past generation and the future generations. I often teach, "Every deed has a seed." In other words, the deeds you choose to do in this lifetime create a seed for future generations. That businessman who takes a trip and watches pornography in secret in his hotel room is not just affecting himself, but he is also sowing seeds for generations to come. Similarly, if that same businessman chooses instead to worship God in the privacy of his hotel room, seeds of worship and faith are being sown into the future generations. Wherever you go, every deed is producing a seed. You're either sowing iniquity for the next generation, or you're sowing equity, spiritually and righteously, for the next generation. Today, pray for those in your family and those yet to come. Break generational curses and establish blessings. Lay a foundation for the next generation. (See Isaiah 58.)

Prayer targets for my family today:

_____

_____

_____

_____

_____

_____

> May the LORD bless you from Zion
> all the days of your life; may you see
> the prosperity of Jerusalem, and may
> you live to see your children's children.
> —Psalm 128:5–6, NIV

DAY 10: Every Assignment Has a Birthplace

I AM CONVINCED THAT we will never walk in the perfect will of God until we seek Him through fasting. God knows your hunger, but He also knows that what you need is living water and the Bread of Life. Taste and see that the Lord is good! Every assignment God gives you has a birthplace. What will He reveal to you today?

Perhaps you are at a place of such desperation that you just cannot afford to miss God's will for your life. I have known people who were literally facing life-or-death situations. They were trapped, they were under pressure by circumstances, and they were under attack by the enemy. The only possible way to survive was to draw near to God—from whose hand no one can snatch you—to hear His voice, and to follow His plan.

Jehoshaphat, king of Judah, was in a similarly critical situation. He was a God-fearing king who found himself surrounded by a powerful enemy army. Annihilation was certain without the Lord's intervention. Scripture records that, "Jehoshaphat feared, and set himself to seek the LORD, and proclaimed a fast throughout all Judah. So Judah gathered together to ask help from the LORD; and from all the cities of Judah they came to seek the LORD....Now all Judah, with their little ones, their wives, and their children, stood before the LORD" (2 Chron. 20:3–4, 13).

All of Judah fasted, even the women and children. They desperately needed to know the Lord's plan to defeat this great enemy army. In the midst of that assembly of fasting people, God spoke to His people through a prophet, who encouraged them, saying, "'Do not be afraid nor dismayed because of this great multitude, for the battle is not yours, but God's....You will not need to fight in this battle. Position yourselves, stand still and see the salvation of the LORD, who is with you, O Judah and Jerusalem!' Do not fear or be dismayed; tomorrow go out against them, for the LORD is with you" (vv. 15, 17).

In the midst of the whole assembly, God told Judah exactly how that enemy army would approach and exactly what they were to do in response. They gave tremendous praise to the Lord, and He set ambushes against the enemy army and defeated them. None escaped. When the people of Judah arrived, it took them three whole days to carry away the spoil!

Do you want God to tell you what you need to do at this time in your life? Fast, worship, and seek Him. Be still and see the salvation of the Lord! They didn't even have to fight. God fought for them. The battle took one day, and God not only delivered them, but He also prospered them. It took them three days to carry off all the riches! I'm ready for some of those victories where it takes me longer to bring the victory home than it took to fight the battle! Press in like Jehoshaphat in times of great distress—you and your whole family, perhaps even your entire church. God will deliver you and show you His plan!

> Let us be filled with the Bread of Life
> instead of the refuse of religion. Begin
> to make fasting a regular discipline, and
> see how God answers your hunger!

On your tenth day of fasting, remember:

◊ Pray and stay in God's Word.

◊ Continue to meditate and listen.

◊ Hunger pangs continue.

Thoughts for your journal:

◇ What do you currently desire in your life? Remember to pray about your dreams and ask God for guidance in what is best for your life.

◇ At this point, what specific assignments do you believe God has for your life?

_____

_____

_____

_____

_____

PRAYER FOCUS DAY 10: Protection

BECAUSE OF JESUS, you and I can take hold of God's promises to protect us, to provide for all our needs, and to cover us in His love, mercy, and grace. He is our *El Shaddai*. He shows Himself strong on our behalf, but He also tenderly takes us unto Himself and shows us kindness. Meditate on these verses of Scripture today, relating to the divine protection of our loving Father.

> You yourselves have seen what I did to Egypt, and how I carried you on eagles' wings and brought you to myself. Now

if you obey me fully and keep my covenant, then out of all
nations you will be my treasured possession.

—EXODUS 19:4–5, NIV

For you have been my refuge, a strong tower against the foe.
I long to dwell in your tent forever and take refuge in the
shelter of your wings. For you have heard my vows, O God;
you have given me the heritage of those who fear your name.

—PSALM 61:3–5, NIV

As a mother comforts her child, so will I comfort you; and
you will be comforted over Jerusalem.

—ISAIAH 66:13, NIV

What is God saying to you today about His protection?

_____

_____

_____

_____

> The name of the LORD is a strong tower;
> the righteous run to it and are safe.
> —Proverbs 18:10

DAY 11: Fasting Truly Humbles You

MOST OF THE fasts mentioned in the Bible were public fasts initiated by the priests; Jesus gave us the model for private fasts in Matthew 6:16–18; 9:14–15. But, public or private, simply stated, fasting is a biblical way to truly humble yourself in the sight of God.

If Jesus needed to fast, how much greater is our need to fast? I was seventeen years old when I went on my first complete twenty-one-day fast. It was one of the most difficult things I had ever done. Fasting is never easy. Honestly, I know of nothing more wearisome than fasting. Jesus understands the difficulty of depriving ourselves of food. In Hebrews 4:15 we read, "For we do not have a High Priest who cannot sympathize with our weaknesses, but was in all points tempted as we are, yet without sin." He also provides strength for us to overcome temptation in Hebrews 4:16: "Let us therefore come boldly to the throne of grace, that we may obtain mercy and find grace to help in time of need." With these promises in mind, the process became less unpleasant for me.

When you fast, you abstain from food for spiritual purposes. I have heard people say that they were planning to fast TV or computer games or surfing the Internet. It is good to put those things down if they are interfering with your prayer life or with your study of God's Word or your ministering to the needs of others, but technically, that is not fasting. Fasting is doing without food for a period of time, which generally causes you to leave the commotion of normal activity. Part of the sacrifice of fasting, seeking God, and studying His Word is that normal activity fades into the background.

There are wrong reasons to fast. You do not fast to obtain merit with God or to get rid of sin. There is only one thing that gives us merit with God and cleanses us of sin—the blood of Jesus. However, fasting will begin to bring to the surface any areas of compromise in your life and make you more aware of any sin in your own life so you can repent.

Fasting is not a Christian diet. You should not fast to lose weight, although weight loss is a normal side effect. Unless you put prayer with your fasting, there is no need to fast. Merely doing without food is just starving. When you fast, you focus on prayer and on God's Word.

You can always find a reason not to fast, so you have to make up your mind that you are going to do it, and everything else will take care of itself. If you will determine to set apart the first days of the year to fast, you will set the course for the entire coming year, and God will add blessings to your life all year long. Just as you set the course of your day by meeting with God in the first hours, the same is true of dedicating the first days of the year to fasting.

King David said, "I humbled myself with fasting" (Ps. 35:13; see also Ezra 8:21).

> God desires to move powerfully in your life.
>
> His plans for you are always progressing
>
> and developing. He desires to speak to
>
> you, as one would speak to a friend.

On your eleventh day of fasting, remember:

- ◇ Rest and relax.
- ◇ Go to your prayer time and prayer place.
- ◇ The Lord's presence becomes more apparent.

Thoughts for your journal:

◊ Humility is a discipline and not something that just comes
naturally. Fasting places one truly in the hands of God, depen-
dent upon Him for spiritual nourishment in the absence
of physical nourishment. Journal how this experience has
humbled you and made you trust God more.

_____

_____

_____

_____

_____

PRAYER FOCUS DAY 11: Favor

WHEN YOU TRULY grasp the concept of God's favor, of His capacity,
you will never be the same. You see, when you offer God a cup,
He not only fills it, as David said, but He also overflows it (Ps. 23:5). God's
"capacity" is unlimited and cannot be exhausted. In the second chapter of
Acts, the Holy Spirit didn't merely "enter" the room; He "filled the whole
house where they were sitting" (v. 2). So whatever you are believing God for
during this fast, I encourage you to believe Him for the *maximum*. Believe
Him for His favor…for *His measure* of capacity, not your own. Rise up and

confront the barriers standing in your way. Do not allow circumstances to dictate your territory limitations—your territory is expanding!

Places I am experiencing the favor of the Lord and the expansion of my "territory":

_____

_____

_____

_____

_____

> I tell you, now is the time of God's
> favor, now is the day of salvation.
> —2 Corinthians 6:2, NIV
>
> Offer to God thanksgiving, and pay
> your vows to the Most High.
> Call upon Me in the day of trouble;
> I will deliver you, and you
> shall glorify Me.
> —Psalm 50:14–15

T HE HOLY SPIRIT is using your fast to reveal your true spiritual condition, resulting in brokenness, repentance, and a transformed life. God looks throughout the earth for those faithful few upon whom He can pour out His blessing in extraordinary ways. When you fast, you attract His attention as one willing to venture beyond the norms of religion and into the great adventure.

The Hebrew root for *sanctify* is *qadhash*, which is also the root for *holy*. God said: "I am the LORD your God; consecrate yourselves and be holy, because I am holy" (Lev. 11:44, NIV). Sanctification is the process of becoming holy in daily life; it is practicing purity and being set apart from the world and from sin. Sanctification is allowing the Holy Spirit to make us more like Jesus in what we do, in what we think, and in what we desire. We do not hear much about sanctification from the pulpits these days, but if we are to see God do wonders in our midst, we must confront sin in our lives and live holy.

God was about to lead His chosen people out against the enemies of God, but they could not stand if they were not holy. This is clearly seen in the contrast between Israel's supernatural victory against the city of Jericho (Josh. 6), and their defeat in Joshua 7 by the tiny army of Ai after Israel had sinned by having stolen things in their midst.

We desire to be in the will of God and to walk according to His plans. Sanctification is the key to being in God's will. As Paul said, "For this is the will of God, your sanctification" (1 Thess. 4:3). There is no need to try to find some mysterious "wheel of God" out there. You cannot follow God's leading until you start where Paul said to start.

Fasting is an essential means of sanctifying yourself, pulling yourself away from the world, and getting closer to God. Fasting allows you to filter your life and to set yourself apart to seek the Lord. Jesus prayed for us:

They are not of the world, just as I am not of the world. Sanctify them by Your truth. Your word is truth. As You sent Me into the world, I also have sent them into the world. And for their sakes I sanctify Myself, that they also may be sanctified by the truth.

—JOHN 17:16–19

Fasting will help you identify areas of even hidden sin and things that are displeasing to God in your life. Fasting helps you discern between serving the flesh and serving the spirit. "For if the blood of bulls and goats and the ashes of a heifer, sprinkling the unclean, sanctifies for the purifying of the flesh, how much more shall the blood of Christ, who through the eternal Spirit offered Himself without spot to God, cleanse your conscience from dead works to serve the living God?" (Heb. 9:13–14). If we are in Christ, His blood cleanses us from dead works, enabling us to serve God in holiness.

> Fasting helps you distinguish between what you want and what you really need. When you choose not to worry about these things and to seek Him first, you are demonstrating the kind of faith that is pleasing to God, because you are trusting Him to also give you all the things that you need.

On your twelfth day of fasting, remember:

⬦ Journal your daily thoughts.

⬦ Continue to focus on God.

⬦ Hunger is still an issue, but stay focused.

Thoughts for your journal:

⬦ What has God revealed to you personally?

⬦ Reflect on what it means to present your body as a living sacrifice through your time of fasting.

PRAYER FOCUS DAY 12: Right Relationships and Kingdom Connections

PEOPLE CAN BE used in our lives as blessings of God or as tools of the enemy. You have to be able to "discern" the difference between the two. There are "flesh people" who tear you down, but there are "faith people" who build you up and help you unlock your potential. "Flesh people" feed your fear and cause you to feel like you've lost your dream. The "right relationships" begin to instill in you a can-do attitude. You begin to stretch your thinking: "Well, maybe I can do that." You can be "catapulted" by the relationships that God puts in your life. So, as you continue to fast and press in to Him today, seek His counsel on the relationships in your life. Which ones are draining? Which ones are supporting you? Which do you represent to others?

_____

_____

_____

_____

_____

_____

> My sheep hear my voice, and I
> know them, and they follow Me.
> —John 10:27

DAY 13: Hold on to the Promise

GOD IS A rewarder of those who diligently seek Him, which means He has already laid up rewards for you in heaven. Now, I've always read that scripture the wrong way. In my mind, I've always added, "seek Him...*and find Him.*" But the Bible tells us that if we *seek*, we *will* find. God will not allow you to give in to temptation. He is with you. Remember your dream to complete the fast, and keep your feet on the path of righteousness. You are over halfway there!

For ten years and two hundred thirty episodes, the TV sitcom *Friends* became a focal point for millions in this country. In 1994, the critics said this show about six young single friends living in New York City was not very entertaining, clever, or original. The final episode of that show had 52 million viewers. The critics who said it wouldn't make it didn't take into account the great vacuum for connection in American culture. People want and need to be connected in relationships.

That need to be connected is evidenced in the church by home groups and a greater emphasis on community. While that is good, if we're not careful, we can become too horizontally focused and not sufficiently vertically focused. Church right now, for the most part in the Western world, particularly in America, is all about *me*: "I want my needs met. Bless me; teach me; help me." While those are legitimate needs and desires, we must keep in mind that the cross has two beams: one is horizontal—but the other is vertical.

Fasting turns your priorities more vertical and more in line with God's desires. It's what Jesus did when He cleared the temple. They had become excessively horizontal.

> Then Jesus went into the temple of God and drove out all
> those who bought and sold in the temple, and overturned the

tables of the money changers and the seats of those who sold doves. And He said to them, "It is written, 'My house shall be called a house of prayer,' but you have made it a 'den of thieves.'"

—MATTHEW 21:12–13

That doesn't mean that when you fast, you don't have specific needs and desires of your own for which you are seeking God. Indeed, you should fast for a specific purpose. However, I believe that as you continue on a prolonged fast, the true cry of your heart becomes, "More of You, God, and less of me." When you put Him first, all else is added.

According to God's principle of "first things," what you put first will order the rest. When you put your spirit first, you serve the things of the Holy Spirit rather than the desires of the flesh. As a result, your mind, will, emotions, as well as your physical body and health will fall in line according to the Spirit's leading. "For if you live according to the flesh you will die; but if by the Spirit you put to death the deeds of the body, you will live" (Rom. 8:13).

> When we fast, we are effectively going on a hunger strike against hell to say, "Loose those who are bound by deception, lies, alcohol, drugs, pornography, false religion, etc!"

On your thirteenth day of fasting, remember:

- ◇ Keep water with you at all times.

- ◇ Continue to meditate and listen.

- ◇ Cravings may return.

Thoughts for your journal:

- ◇ What are the various ways you can experience guidance from God?

- ◇ Reflect on how you can resist more temptation in these next days as the hunger pangs continue.

PRAYER FOCUS DAY 13: Body of Christ

CHRISTIANS ALL OVER the world need prayer. In China, believers meet in secret locations in the underground church. If they are discovered, they risk being beaten, tortured, imprisoned, and worse for their faith. In Ethiopia, believers are brutally attacked and suffer greatly when they refuse to renounce Jesus. In other hostile and closed regions, like Cuba and Vietnam, brave believers share the Word of God with others at great personal risk. Even in our "Christian" nation, the cross of Christ and our beliefs are constantly under attack. So, on this thirteenth day of your fast, concentrate in prayer on the body of Christ—those who are suffering and persecuted for their faith, those who are struggling to hold on to their faith, and those whom the devil wishes to pick off from our younger generation.

Prayer targets within the body of Christ:

_____

_____

_____

_____

_____

> But God composed the body, having given greater honor to that part which lacks it, that there should be no schism in the body, but that the members should have the same care for one another. And if one member suffers, all the members suffer with it; or if one member is honored, all the members rejoice with it.
> —1 Corinthians 12:24–26

DAY 14: Magnifying Your Worship

W HAT DID DAVID mean when he said, "Deep calls unto deep," in Psalm 42:7? While fasting, David's hunger and thirst for God was greater than his natural desire for food. As a result, he reached a place where he could cry out from the depths of his spirit to the depths of God, even in the midst of his trial. Once you've experienced even a glimpse of that kind of intimacy with the Holy Creator of the universe—and the countless rewards and blessings that follow—your worship life changes.

David was a man after God's heart. He was a man who fasted often, and not just from food. As a youth, he was often in the fields alone with just the sheep and his God. After he was anointed king, he spent many days running for his life. David wrote Psalm 34 while alone and on the run from Saul in the land of the Philistines. But David stirred himself to worship God even in those conditions, proclaiming, "His praise shall continually be in my mouth" (v. 1), and "taste and see that the LORD is good" (v. 8). A routine worshiper in those circumstances would have been totally overwhelmed. But David knew that to worship God was to magnify God. His invitation to all of us to "magnify the LORD with me" (v. 3) still stands open today.

What would your answer be if the Lord asked you, "Do you remember the last time you were lovesick for Me?" I began to ponder that question recently. I thought back to the time when Cherise and I were dating. We were deeply in love and wanted to spend every moment together. It was probably a good thing our parents wouldn't let us because we would have surely starved to death. For the longest time, whenever we would go out to eat, we would end up talking after about three bites because we were so engrossed with each other. I know that sounds a little sappy, but stay with me—I have a point. I cannot tell you the money I wasted on meals, simply because our desire to talk and spend time with each other was greater than our desire for food. We were "lovesick" for each other. As I thought back on that, it hit me. That is what the Lord feels when we fast. When we are so lovesick for our first love, fasting is easy.

So I ask you, do you remember the last time you walked away from a meal because you were so preoccupied with your first love that the food was of no interest? Have you experienced seasons when it felt like the Bridegroom was distant? You just don't sense His presence as close as you once did. You have no heart for worship, and you lack the excitement and childlike enthusiasm you once had for spiritual things. Perhaps it is time to stop the busyness of your everyday life and declare a fast, a season of lovesickness to restore the passion of your first love back to its proper place in your life. When you fast, everything slows down. The days seem longer. The nights seem longer, but in the quietness of seeking, you will find Him whom your heart desires.

When you worship, you magnify God. Your enemies or circumstances may seem to be so large and so powerful that they are all you can see. But when you worship, you not only magnify God but you also reduce the size and power of everything else around you. Later in Psalm 34, David said, "I sought the LORD, and He heard me, and delivered me from all my fears" (v. 4). God will hear you when you set your heart to worship Him. When you magnify the Lord, you shrink the supposed power of your enemy, the devil. The greatest thing you can do in the midst of a battle is magnify the Lord. Jehoshaphat is proof of that. When under attack, the whole nation cried out, fasted, and worshiped God. Jehoshaphat sent the praisers out ahead of the army to magnify their God, and He utterly delivered Judah from their enemy.

> God does not need our routines or savor
> heartless activity. He does not want our
> "leftovers." True worship that comes from
> our hearts feeds Him and satisfies Him; it
> is something He desires—and deserves.

On your fourteenth day of fasting, remember:

- ◊ Listen to your favorite worship CDs.
- ◊ Focus on your meditation and listening for God's still, small voice.
- ◊ Weight loss continues.

Thoughts for your journal:

- ◊ Praise God for bringing you this far, and thank Him for His steadfast presence.

_____

_____

_____

_____

_____

DISCERNMENT IS THE ability to judge rightly. Just as Solomon prayed for wisdom, you and I can ask God to strengthen our discernment of people, situations, and opportunities. It has to do with being sensitive to His Spirit, which increases exponentially when you are fasting. So, as you continue this journey, make it a point of prayer to ask God to increase your discernment of people, situations, and more. And study His Word. As the writer of Hebrews reminds us, "For the word of God is living and powerful, and sharper than any two-edged sword, piercing even to the division of soul and spirit, and of joints and marrow, and is a discerner of the thoughts and intents of the heart" (Heb. 4:12).

Dear friends, do not believe every
spirit, but test the spirits to see whether
they are from God, because many false
prophets have gone out into the world.
—1 John 4:1, NIV

I F JESUS COULD have accomplished all He came to do without fasting, why did He fast? The Son of God fasted because He knew there were supernatural things that could only be released that way. How much more should fasting be common practice in our lives?

Fasting is not a means to promote yourself. The greatest thing fasting will do for you will be to break down all of the stuff that accumulates from this world that blocks you from clear communion with the Father. You have to make time to get away and pray, whether you feel like it or not. Fasting in and of itself is a continual prayer to God. You are praying twenty-four hours a day when you are fasting. If you have been fasting all day, you've been praying all day.

Some of the greatest miracles, breakthroughs, and seasons of prayer I have ever experienced did not come when I was "feeling led" to pray and fast. They actually came when the last thing I wanted to do was drag myself to my prayer place, but I did, and God honored my faithfulness. Jesus said, "When you pray…when you fast…when you give…" (Matt. 6). He expects those who follow Him to do these things whether feeling a special *leading* or not. These things should be part of every believer's life.

As you fast, target your unsaved loved ones in prayer. Create a "hit list" of people you want to see saved. It is good to be very specific in your prayers during a fast. What is the one most critical thing you want God to do in your life? God told Habakkuk to "write the vision and make it plain" (Hab. 2:2). I dare you to write down the names of those you want to see saved, and when you fast and pray, call those names out to God. As we have seen evidenced here at Free Chapel, I believe you too will see breakthroughs like you never dreamed possible!

If you let it, your flesh will take over and rule your life. That is why times of fasting are so crucial to your walk with God. Fasting helps you establish dominion and authority over your flesh. "Do not be deceived, God is not mocked; for whatever a man sows, that he will also reap. For he who sows to his flesh will of the flesh reap corruption, but he who sows to the Spirit will of the Spirit reap everlasting life. And let us not grow weary while doing good, for in due season we shall reap if we do not lose heart" (Gal. 6:7–9). Keep your armor fit and your blade sharp!

What was your reason for starting this fast? Have you had a spiritual awakening?

> Whether you desire to be closer to God or are
> in need of great breakthroughs in your life,
> remember that nothing shall be impossible for
> you. Fasting is truly a secret source of power!

On your fifteenth day of fasting, remember:

◊ Stay hydrated.

◊ Be sure to listen to God as you pray.

◊ You become mentally aware of the Lord's presence all around you.

Thoughts for your journal:

◊ Reflect on how worship and obedience have provided you with the opportunity for God to reveal Himself and His purposes to you, His special servant.

◇ Write down the details that were a concern in the beginning of the fast that no longer seem of great concern.

_____

_____

_____

_____

_____

_____

PRAYER FOCUS DAY 15: Revealing Giftings (Personal and Spiritual)

WHEN YOU READ Paul's letters, you see that he kept around him people of different backgrounds and people with different gifts. In other words, he had some people who were gifted at hospitality. He had some people whose main contribution was prayer. No matter what the gift is, it must be opened. It is to bless you and others around you. God has given you unique and special divine enablements; gifts, as it were. Are you using them to glorify Him and advance His kingdom? Have you fully discovered what those gifts are yet? Today, ask God to show you what your giftings—both personal and spiritual—may be.

_____

_____

_____

_____

_____

_____

As each one has received a gift,
minister it to one another, as good
stewards of the manifold grace of God.
—1 Peter 4:10

DAY 16: Purest Worship

THE DISCIPLINE OF fasting breaks you out of the world's routine. It is a form of worship—offering your body to God as a living sacrifice is holy and pleasing to God (Rom. 12:1). The discipline of fasting will humble you, remind you of your dependency on God, and bring you back to your first love. It causes the roots of your relationship with Jesus, and your worship, to go deeper.

Heaviness drains worship out of your life. Church is depressing unless you learn to worship. I know that is a strange statement, but it is true. There is nothing worse than a Spirit-filled church that loses the garment of praise and picks up the spirit of heaviness. God desires our praise more than our mere church attendance. That is not to say we should forsake assembling together as a corporate body. But our times together, just as our times alone, should be to glorify and praise our awesome, mighty God. Praise pushes back the enemy!

One of my favorite examples of this fact is found in 2 Chronicles. King Jehoshaphat is told "'a great multitude is coming against you from beyond the sea, from Syria; and they are in Hazazon Tamar' (which is En Gedi). And Jehoshaphat feared, and set himself to seek the LORD, and proclaimed a fast throughout all Judah" (2 Chron. 20:2–3).

Now, Jehoshaphat had just gotten the kingdom of Judah in order. Things were going well. No sooner did they start enjoying that peace when they heard that an army—far larger than they could defeat on their own—was already on its way. Jehoshaphat could have died under that spirit of heaviness. The scripture says that he "feared," but he only paused a moment there. He immediately set himself and all the people of Judah to seek the Lord through fasting and prayer. Then he took his place in the assembly of the people and began to praise—proclaiming who God was and all that God had done for them. He ended by saying, "We have no power against this great multitude that is coming against us; nor do we know what to do, but our eyes are upon You" (v. 12). Then they waited.

How many times do we find ourselves saying that same thing: "I don't know what to do. This problem is far too big for me to handle." We must put our eyes on God! The story continues: "Then the Spirit of the LORD came upon Jahaziel…a Levite of the sons of Asaph, in the midst of the assembly" (2 Chron. 20:14). God told them that the battle was not theirs but His. He told them exactly where the enemy would be, but He said, "'You will not need to fight in this battle. Position yourselves, stand still and see the salvation of the LORD, who is with you, O Judah and Jerusalem!' Do not fear or be dismayed; tomorrow go out against them, for the LORD is with you" (v. 17).

I don't know about you, but realizing that the Lord was going to destroy my enemies would be reason enough to shout! And that is just what the people of Judah did. Young and old "stood up to praise the LORD God of Israel with voices loud and high." The next day, they went early to the place the Lord had directed them. Then Jehoshaphat addressed the people again saying:

> "Hear me, O Judah and you inhabitants of Jerusalem: Believe in the LORD your God, and you shall be established; believe His prophets, and you shall prosper." And when he had consulted with the people, he appointed those who should sing to the LORD, and who should praise the beauty of holiness, as they went out before the army and were saying: Praise the LORD, for His mercy endures forever.
> —2 CHRONICLES 20:20–21

Now, notice what happened when they began to praise: "The LORD set ambushes against the people of Ammon, Moab, and Mount Seir, who had come against Judah; and they were defeated" (v. 22).

There is power in corporate fasting and power in corporate praise! It creates a river of healing, a river of deliverance and victory, a river of cleansing in the house of God. It is time to exchange ashes for beauty, mourning for joy, and a garment of heaviness for a garment of praise.

> The discipline of fasting breaks you out of the world's routine. It is a form of worship—offering your body to God as a living sacrifice is holy and pleasing to God (Rom. 12:1).

On your sixteenth day of fasting, remember:

- ◊ Observe your prayer time and prayer place.
- ◊ Reflect on your fast and how it is helping you to grow spiritually.
- ◊ Your senses become more sensitive to your surroundings and the voice of God.

Thoughts for your journal:

- ◊ Remember to stay the course. Write out your thoughts on how you can continue to present your body as a living sacrifice, and see if the Lord does not open up the windows of heaven to you and shower you with His presence.
- ◊ Fasting is a form of worship that will humble you. Remind yourself of your dependency on God.

GOD HAS GIVEN you giftings to use for His purposes. It makes me think of Abraham and the five dynamics that brought him into the place of ministry, the place of destiny that God had for him. First, he could "hear" God. Second, Abraham believed what he heard. Third, he came to a place of denouncing the comfort zone he lived in, in order to follow God's leading. Fourth, Abraham had the courage to follow God's direction for his life. And finally, he had the tenacity to focus on the promise and not the problems that stood in his way. So, on this day of the fast, I encourage you to pray and seek God about His purpose and plan for your life, your ministry unto Him.

_____

_____

_____

_____

Then Jesus said to His disciples,
"If anyone wishes to come after
Me, he must deny himself, and
take up his cross and follow Me."
—Matthew 16:24, NASU

GOD DESIRES TO move powerfully in your life. His plans for you are always progressing and developing. He desires to speak to you, as one would speak to a friend. That's how He spoke with Abraham. We must get to the place where we are desperate for God again. We must begin to desire Him more than food or drink. Let us be filled with the bread of presence instead of the refuse of religion.

The eleventh chapter of the Book of Hebrews is often referred to as "the hall of faith," beginning with the words, "Now faith is the substance of things hoped for, the evidence of things not seen" (Heb. 11:1). Some of the most encouraging words in the Bible are found in this book. It is said that after the birth of Seth to Adam and Eve, people began to call on the name of the Lord (Gen. 4:26). Enoch was born many years later, and his life went a step beyond merely calling on the name of the Lord. Thousands of years after his departure from this earth, the writer of the Book of Hebrews said of him: "By faith Enoch was translated that he should not see death; and was not found, because God had translated him: for before his translation he had this testimony, that he pleased God" (Heb. 11:5, KJV).

What was it about Enoch that was different from those before him? What about his life was so pleasing to God? The answer is found in Hebrews:

> But without faith it is impossible to please him: for he that cometh to God must believe that he is, and that he is a rewarder of them that diligently seek him.
> —HEBREWS 11:6, KJV

Enoch knew God. Not only that, but Genesis 5:22 also says that Enoch "walked with God" for three hundred years! Now, if I were to choose what could be said of me, I would want my testimony to be "he pleased God." Notice that Enoch did not try to please people. In fact, Jude records that

Enoch prophesied in a manner that would have made him very unpopular with the party crowd (Jude 14–15). Enoch's primary concern was walking in faith, which is what pleases God. According to Hebrews 11:6, it is reasonable to say that Enoch came to God, he believed God, he diligently sought God, and he was rewarded.

If you want to please God, *believe* God. Take Him at His Word. When the apostle Paul was teaching the Corinthians, a knowledge-seeking society, he told them, "We walk by faith, not by sight" (2 Cor. 5:7). Shadrach, Meshach, and Abednego walked by faith and not by sight. The three of them joined Daniel in his initial fast from the king's delicacies. Think about what they saw on their way into that furnace. It had been heated seven times hotter than normal. The heat was so intense that it killed the guards standing by the doors. If they had walked by sight, they would have said, "Today we shall surely be ashes." Instead, by faith, they walked on, saying, "Our God whom we serve is able to deliver us from the burning fiery furnace, and He will deliver us from your hand, O king" (Dan. 3:17). Faith is the evidence of things unseen.

> Jesus put the emphasis on how great our God is, not how great our faith is. With only a tiny bit of faith, like a mustard seed, we can move mountains, and nothing shall be impossible.

On your seventeenth day of fasting, remember:

◊ Listen to worship music for inspiration and support.

- Reflect on your fast and how it is helping you to grow spiritually.
- Cravings are apparent.

Thoughts for your journal:

- Reflect on those situations from God's Word that seemed impossible but for the power of God.
- What situations in your life seem impossible and need God's touch?

PRAYER FOCUS DAY 17: Mentors and Discipleship

A S THEY WERE going along the road, someone said to Him, 'I will follow You wherever You go'" (Luke 9:57, NASU). It is one thing to say you will follow Jesus; it is another to see it through, even when the road is narrow, steep, and nearly impossible. We all need fathers and mothers in the faith who have walked the road with Jesus and can gently help us along at times. These mentors are invaluable when they are of the Lord. Pray today that God will bring right relationships into your life…fathers and mothers in the faith who can strengthen you and build you up.

_____

_____

_____

_____

_____

_____

> It was he who gave some to be apostles, some to be prophets, some to be evangelists, and some to be pastors and teachers, to prepare God's people for works of service, so that the body of Christ may be built up until we all reach unity in the faith and in the knowledge of the Son of God and become mature, attaining to the whole measure of the fullness of Christ.
> —Ephesians 4:11–13, NIV

GOD DOESN'T WANT you to worry. He wants to be in control of your life and guide you through your daily challenges. As you are fasting and giving God your body, give Him your spirit too.

Someone once sent me a mustard seed from Israel. Just to put things into perspective, a butter bean seed is about four hundred times bigger than a mustard seed, but it will yield only a small bush. On the other hand, a common mustard seed is only about one millimeter in diameter, and it grows into a small tree. The more common mustard plants are perennial, growing back year after year and developing deeper root systems each season. You could try to pull one of these little trees out of the ground, but the stems would most likely break, leaving the roots to regenerate a new plant.

That is the type of faith we are to have! Jesus put the emphasis on how great our God is, not how great our faith is. With only a tiny bit of faith, like a mustard seed, we can move mountains, and nothing shall be impossible.

As Christians, we need to stop measuring our faith by the size of the problem. We need to start looking instead at how great our God is. We need to plant that seed of faith—no matter how small—into whatever mountain stands in our way and believe it will be moved, because Jesus said it would.

When Peter tried to walk on water, he made it only a few steps because he took his eyes off Jesus, and fear dragged him down.

When he began to sink, Jesus lifted him up out of the water and said, "You of little faith" (Matt. 14:31). Peter did have little faith because that is what it took to walk on water.

If he could do that with just a little faith, imagine what will happen when that faith increases!

In the closing chapter of the Book of Hebrews, the writer tells us, "Remember your leaders, who spoke the word of God to you. Consider the outcome of their way of life and imitate their faith" (Heb. 13:7, NIV). As I asked before, if our Lord fasted, why would we think that we should not fast? There is no record of Jesus ever healing anyone until He returned from the forty days of fasting that launched His earthly ministry. Jesus said we would do even greater works than He did, because He was returning to the Father. If Jesus did not begin to minister before fasting, how can we?

> Satan gets disturbed—and defeated—
> when you decide to do more than be a
> Sunday-morning Christian. The devil knows
> that fasting releases God's power.

On your eighteenth day of fasting, remember:
- ◊ Pray and stay in God's Word.
- ◊ Continue to journal your experiences.
- ◊ Meditate on what this fast means to you.

Thoughts for your journal:
- ◊ Examine any areas of unforgiveness and bitterness that the Lord is asking you to surrender to Him.

_____

_____

_____

_____

_____

_____

_____

PRAYER FOCUS DAY 18: Binding Oppression and Fear

THERE MAY BE times in your life when your enemies or circumstances seem to be so large and so powerful that they are all you can see. In Psalm 69, David is crying out that he was sinking in "deep mire" (v. 2) and the floods were overtaking him. But his heart turned to worship despite his circumstances. When you worship, you not only magnify God, but you also reduce the size and power of everything else around you. God will hear you when you set your heart to worship Him. When you magnify the Lord, you shrink the supposed power of your enemy, the devil. The greatest thing you can do in the midst of a battle is to magnify the Lord. "I will praise the name of God with a song, and will magnify Him with thanksgiving" (Ps. 69:30).

What areas do you need to magnify the Lord
in today?

_____

_____

_____

_____

_____

_____

> Oh, magnify the LORD with me,
> and let us exalt His name together. I
> sought the LORD, and He heard me,
> and delivered me from all my fears.
> —Psalm 34:3–4

DAY 19: Rewarded Openly

WHETHER DONE CORPORATELY or individually, fasting is a personal, private discipline. It is a sacrifice born out of expectancy. Job went through a devastating trial and lost everything. Yet he continued to pray and fast, saying, "I have treasured the words of His mouth more than my necessary food" (Job 23:12). God "restored Job's losses," and "blessed the latter days of Job more than the first," and even gave him more sons and daughters. God's open rewards flooded Job's life.

I want to share with you some of the open rewards that God told me He would pour out on us at Free Chapel as we were diligent to seek Him in giving, praying, and fasting. These same rewards are open to every believer!

First, He told me that fasting will break poverty from your life. As I plant a seed each time I fast, major blessings return on my life. Again looking at Joel 2:15–16, the people were so poor and in such a famine that they couldn't even bring an offering. But God said to "blow the trumpet in Zion, sanctify a fast, call a solemn assembly" (KJV). After that fast, the threshing floor was full of wheat, the oil vats were overflowing, and they ate in plenty and were satisfied. The Lord brought great financial blessing to people who fasted and prayed. When fasting is a lifestyle, poverty will not be.

God also said that health and healing would follow fasting. Of His chosen fast God said, "Then your light shall break forth like the morning, your healing shall spring forth speedily" (Isa. 58:8). Fasting humbles you and brings clarity, even allowing you to get unforgiveness and bitterness out of your heart. Some people have tried and tried to truly forgive someone but have never been able to let the matter go. Begin a fast, and trust God to work that in your heart. Earlier in the book, I told you how fasting helps you physically because it cleanses your body and gives your organs time to rest. It also helps you "spring clean" in a spiritual sense because it makes you sensitive to the desires of the Lord. Unforgiveness, bitterness, and the like can all be linked to illnesses, fatigue, stress, and more.

Fasting will also help you overcome sexual addictions and demonic powers. It will break great sin off people. In Matthew 17:21, Jesus said of that stubborn demon that "this kind does not go out except by prayer and fasting." Remember? Now, we don't wrestle with flesh and blood. But there is a spirit behind homosexuality. There is a spirit behind pornography. There is a spirit behind adultery. There is a spirit behind fornication. These demonic spirits of perversion manipulate and use people like puppets on a string. But fasting will break the stronghold of demonic sexual addictions like pornography, homosexuality, adultery, fornication, and lust.

God will also target your children who are being led off and destroyed by the enemy's devices. In the Book of Joel, God called for a holy fast. And He said, "It shall come to pass afterward that I will pour out My Spirit on all flesh; your sons and your daughters shall prophesy" (Joel 2:28). Many times the rewards of fasting come after the fast, though from time to time answers can come during the fast. Look at the story of Hezekiah's son, Manasseh, who became king of Judah (2 Chron. 33:1–13). Manasseh was a wicked king whom God had warned many times to no avail. Then the army of Assyria captured Hezekiah's son, put a hook in his nose, bound him in chains, and took him to Babylon. In his distress, Manasseh cried out to God and humbled himself with fasting. The Bible says God heard his plea and "brought him back to Jerusalem into his kingdom. Then Manasseh knew that the LORD was God" (v. 13).

The scandals and corruption on the front pages
of our newspapers and the gross perversion
that is prevalent on every level of society tell
us how much we need revival in this country.
How much more should we, as Christians,
devote ourselves to fasting and prayer?

On your nineteenth day of fasting, remember:

◇ Continue to drink water.

◇ Pray for guidance and strength.

◇ Document your thoughts in your journal.

Thoughts for your journal:

◇ Consider what you would be willing to share with others today. How you will articulate your experience, and what it has meant to you in terms of your relationship with God?

REVIVAL IS WHEN Earth is attacked by heaven. Revival is an awesome move of God that affects you in powerful ways. Revival is when you get closer to heaven than you are to anything on Earth. We need revival in America. We need heaven to touch Earth with power. So, as you near the end of your fast, pray for revival. Ask God to send the rain of His Spirit on the land to break up the hardened hearts and bring forth a harvest of souls. Cry out for it as a desperate man crying out for water in the desert. Our young people need revival. We need revival. The church needs revival. In the past, the great revivals were always preceded by seasons of fasting and prayer. Do not grow weary, but stand strong in the power of His might!

LORD, I have heard of your fame;
I stand in awe of your deeds, O
LORD. Renew them in our day,
in our time make them known;
in wrath remember mercy.
—Habakkuk 3:2, NIV

DAY 20: His Will, Not Yours

B Y NOW, YOUR fast has led you through many different emotions and levels of God's presence. You are beginning to see the reward of the humbling of your flesh that can only take place during a fast. You are dying to your own will and desires, and sensing the desires of His heart filling you and prompting you to great things. Continue on this journey!

God's priorities are seldom our priorities. That is the difference in the nature of man and the nature of God. He even said so: "As the heavens are higher than the earth, so are my ways higher than your ways and my thoughts than your thoughts" (Isa. 55:9, NIV). So, how do we position ourselves to hear from God? How do we free ourselves from our own desires, to know His will? Well, I can tell you from firsthand experience that fasting causes you to take that sword of God's Word and separate what you "want" from what you "need."

When you fast and sanctify yourself unto God, it moves you off the bank and into the miracles! There are too many people on the edge of what God is doing, and not enough of us standing firmly in the middle of His will. Do you want things to change in your home? You are the priest of your home—fast, sanctify yourself, and take a firm stand in the middle of God's will! When your family sees you stepping off the edge of mere "Sunday morning religion" and getting right into the middle of what God is doing, they will follow and find God's direction for their lives.

You should be attached to a local body of believers instead of just trying to find your own way. If ever there was a time where we needed to be crossing together, taking a firm, united stand against sin in this nation, it is now. We need each other. We need a spirit of togetherness. We need a spirit of trust. We need a spirit of unity. We need a spirit of compassion for one another.

We desire to be in the will of God and to walk according to His plans.

Sanctification is the key to being in God's will. As Paul said, "For this is the will of God, your sanctification" (1 Thess. 4:3). Fasting is an essential means of sanctifying yourself, pulling yourself away from the world, and getting closer to God. Fasting allows you to filter your life and to set yourself apart to seek the Lord.

> Fasting is what prepares you for a new anointing (Mark 2:20). God can't put that kind of wine in old skins. If you want new wine, new miracles, new closeness, new intimacy with Him, then it's time to call a fast and shed that old skin for the new.

On your twentieth day of fasting, remember:

◊ Pray and stay in God's Word.

◊ Worship God through music and praise.

◊ Cravings are apparent, but you've lasted this long!

Thoughts for your journal:

◊ Take some time today and go back to read your journal entries from the start of the fast to this twentieth day.

- What do your journal entries tell you about your own personal journey these last three weeks?

- Take a moment and journal about the breakthroughs you have experienced or key things the Lord has shown you during the fast. Spend time in prayer and thanksgiving.

PRAYER FOCUS DAY 20: Laborers Into the Harvest Field

GOD SAID, "ASK of Me, and I will give you the nations for Your inheritance, and the ends of the earth for Your possession" (Ps. 2:8). Jesus told us, "Ask the Lord of the harvest, therefore, to send out workers into his harvest field" (Matt. 9:38, NIV). On this twentieth day of your fast, focus your prayers on these two key instructions from heaven. Cry out to God to save multitudes in the valley of decision. Cry out for the lost and hurting, the poor, the addicted. Ask Him to send missionaries, ambassadors of His Word, into the earth.

_____

_____

_____

_____

_____

_____

_____

> The people who sat in darkness
> have seen a great light, and upon
> those who sat in the region and
> shadow of death Light has dawned.
> —Matthew 4:16

JESUS SAID TO His followers, "Whoever hears these sayings of Mine, and does them, I will liken him to a wise man who built his house on the rock" (Matt. 7:24). Today is the final day of your fast. You have heard His Word, and you have obeyed. You are like that wise man with his house upon a rock! Don't give in today. Press in and hear what the Spirit of the Lord would say to you.

Over twenty years ago when the Lord first called me to preach, He showed me some things that were for a time and season yet to come. I could not walk into all of His promises at once, but I knew He would lead me in His will as I was willing to sanctify myself and follow Him. Recently, the Lord has stirred my spirit with a sense that now is the time. It is as if He is saying, "You've prayed about it. You've dreamed about it. You've asked Me for it. You've longed for it. It's been prophesied over you. Prepare yourself."

I traveled back to North Carolina, where I was born and raised. My grandfather still has a home in Middlesex, North Carolina. It is a beautiful mansionlike homestead set on acres of rolling, lush farmland with horses, cattle, even his own private airstrip for his plane. Twenty-eight children were raised in that house over the years, and all of them serve the Lord.

During that special visit back to my roots, my heritage, I spent time each day walking that airstrip and the fields in prayer and communion with God. I felt the Holy Spirit's leading to visit the place down the road where He first called me to preach. I had not been back there in twenty-two years. I went down to that wonderful old Church of God sanctuary and sat down in the very spot of my calling. I can remember like it was yesterday. I was on a three-day fast, and I was crying out, "Oh, God, can You use me? Why are You calling me to preach? I can't do it. I don't know how to preach. I'm afraid. I'm not worthy. I'm not good enough." I was giving Him all the excuses and all the fear. I didn't realize that during that three-day fast I was cutting off the flesh with a sharp knife.

Finally, on the third day, I heard His voice in my spirit say, "I've called you to preach. Go and do what I've called you to do." I said, "Lord, if this is truly Your will, then let my mother confirm it when I get home, even though it's past midnight. Let her be up, and let her confirm it." I was young, and it never hurts to ask for clarity! I walked out of that tiny sanctuary weeping, got into my car, and drove barely a quarter mile home. When I walked back to Mom's bedroom, she was on her knees praying. As soon as I saw her, she whirled around, pointed her finger, and started speaking with stammering lips: "Jentezen, God has called you to preach. Go and do what He has called you to do."

What if you set yourself to diligently seek the Lord, sanctifying yourself with a fast and journey back to the spot where it all began—where He saved you, set you free, filled you with His Spirit, and called you out? I actually physically traveled to that spot, but if you cannot do that, you can go back mentally. You can recall the ancient landmark, that same simplicity, innocence, and dedication with which you first responded to His voice.

Just as Joshua called the children of promise to sanctify themselves—I believe that, likewise, your "tomorrow" is just around the corner. God is going to do wonders in your life, leading you places you have never been before.

> Fasting will bring you into destiny. Fasting will bring you into alignment with God's plan for your life. Now is the time to fast, to seek God diligently, to sanctify yourself, to discern God's priorities, and to walk in His promises. *Go for it!*

On your twenty-first day of fasting, remember:

◊ Find someone and share your experience with that person.

◊ Replenish yourself with liquids, and prepare to ease back into solid food on the twenty-second day.

◊ Be thankful and rejoice.

◊ Write your feelings in your prayer journal.

◊ Anticipation increases regarding what the Lord is doing in your life.

Praise God!

◊ On this final day, ask the Lord to reveal to you if there is any unforgiveness, bitterness, or other hindrances that you have yet to lay fully before your Lord.

◊ Prepare for blessing, harvest, and an anointing like you have never experienced before.

◊ Get ready because the rest of this year will not be like any other before it!

PRAYER FOCUS DAY 21: Spirit of Prayer for the Holy Spirit to Fall

WHY IS THIS the prayer focus on the last day of your fast? Because by now you are so sensitive to the Holy Spirit that you realize nothing else will satisfy. Nothing else will do in a world gone mad. This world needs the touch of God. It needs the sweeping movement of the Holy

Spirit convicting men of sin and drawing them to the cross. But you have to hunger for it. You have to thirst for it. There's a difference between wanting a drink and being thirsty. When you're thirsty, everything in you says, "I've got to have it." And when you get thirsty, He'll pour out His Spirit. So, focus your prayers today on a spirit of prayer to be released in churches and homes across this land, prayer that God will pour out His Holy Spirit and revive us again!

Therefore, having been justified by faith, we have peace with God through our Lord Jesus Christ, through whom also we have access by faith into this grace in which we stand, and rejoice in hope of the glory of God. And not only that, but we also glory in tribulations, knowing that tribulation produces perseverance; and perseverance, character; and character, hope.

—Romans 5:1–4

Conclusion

CONGRATULATIONS! YOU HAVE ENDURED AND FINISHED THE race, and you will never be the same.

Now, as you come out of your fast...

Be careful and ease back into eating solid foods over the next few days to a week. You must give your body time to recover and get used to digesting food again. Even though cravings may be strong the first few days after the fast, pace yourself, and continue drinking plenty of fluids.

Remember the Faith

In the closing chapter of the Book of Hebrews, the writer tells us, "Remember your leaders, who spoke the word of God to you. Consider the outcome of their way of life and imitate their faith" (Heb. 13:7, NIV). As I asked before, if our Lord fasted, why would we think that we should not fast? There is no record of Jesus ever healing anyone until He returned from the forty days of fasting that launched His earthly ministry. Jesus said we would do even greater works than He had done, because He was returning to the Father. If Jesus did not begin to minister before fasting, how can we?

Throughout the history of the Christian church, God has raised up men and women who were willing to dedicate their lives to Him and diligently seek Him through fasting and prayer. Long seasons of fasting are credited for launching such revivals as seen by Evan Roberts, who fasted and prayed for thirteen months for Laos, his country. Healing evangelists like John

Alexander Dowie, John G. Lake, Maria Woodworth-Etter, Smith Wigglesworth, and Kathryn Kuhlman all understood the tremendous power of faith through fasting in operation throughout their ministries.

There may be times when you are fasting, praying, and standing in faith, yet you still do not sense that anything is happening; there's no "sprout" showing through the dirt. Remember the faith of those before you. David said, "I humbled myself with fasting; and my prayer would return to my own heart. I paced about as though he were my friend or brother; I bowed down heavily, as one who mourns for his mother" (Ps. 35:13–14).

Do not let the enemy drag you down with discouragement. Remember, God gives you the garment of praise for the spirit of heaviness. Sometimes you will not feel like praying when you are fasting, but pray anyway. You will be amazed how God will show up, and it will be like all of heaven has come down and glory has filled your soul.

In this same psalm, David had not yet received an answer to his prayer, yet he is able to wait in faith, proclaiming the praises of God: "Let the LORD be magnified, who has pleasure in the prosperity of His servant. And my tongue shall speak of Your righteousness and of Your praise all the day long" (Ps. 35:27–28). The Lord will reward your diligence; His delight is in the prosperity—the wholeness—of His children.

Also, remember the faith of Abraham: "The substance of things hoped for, the evidence of things not seen" (Heb. 11:1). It was that faith that was credited to him as righteousness—because he *believed* God. Even though Abraham's body was dead as far as fathering children was concerned, he desired a child of his own. God desired it even more and gave him the promise of not only a son but also descendants more numerous than the stars of the sky (Gen. 15:4–6). When you believe Him for some*thing*, you are exercising faith, which pleases God.

Twelve Steps to Victory

Battles will rage long after you have completed your fast. Some things you lay hold of during the fast will require further diligence to see victory.

To help you "stay the course" in the days after your fast—and throughout the year—remember these twelve points and apply them to your life to see the victory of the Lord come to pass in your circumstances.

1. Make it hard on God and easy on you. Take the pressure off yourself to make things happen, because that's God's job (Matt. 11:28; John 5:40; 6:29).

2. Keep on swinging. Don't settle for partial victory (2 Tim. 4:7–8).

3. God says, "When you approach a door that is very large, do not fear, because I will open it." When God opens the door, no man can shut it (Rev. 3:7–8).

4. Don't move in the dark. If you don't know God's will, don't move (Ps. 46:10; Exod. 14:13; Ruth 3:18).

5. Be strong and very courageous. If you lack courage, pray (Phil. 4:6–7).

6. Don't do anything until you ask the Lord first. He will give you a clear word (Eph. 2:10).

7. Don't ask how much it costs; ask God if He wants it done. If so, He'll take care of the cost (2 Cor. 9:8; 3 John 2).

8. Be patient. God loves the last-minute save! "Whoever believes will not act hastily" (Isa. 28:16).

9. Don't stick to sensible methods. If the Lord tells you to do something, do it (Prov. 3:5–6; Isa. 25:3–4)!

10. Practice the John the Baptist factor: "He must increase, but I must decrease" (John 3:30; Phil. 1:21).

11. Look out! you haven't seen anything yet when you mix faith with the Word of God (Hab. 2:4; Rom. 10:17).

12. P-U-S-H: Pray Until Something Happens *or* Praise Until Something Happens (Ps. 149; 2 Chron. 20:21–22; Heb. 13:15).